CHINESE
DOMESTIC FURNITURE

IN PHOTOGRAPHS AND MEASURED DRAWINGS

by Gustav Ecke

DOVER PUBLICATIONS, INC., NEW YORK

TO MY GODCHILD

LEONORE CLARITA

This Dover edition, first published in 1986, is an unabridged republication of the portfolio *Chinese Domestic Furniture*, originally published by Editions Henri Vetch, Peking, 1944, in an edition of 200 copies. A new Publisher's Note, prepared specially for the present edition, provides a physical description of the original portfolio, describes the alterations in pagination in the present edition, and supplies new translations of the Chinese material. The table of contents is heavily revised.

The publisher is grateful to the Department of Special Collections, Stanford University Libraries, for making their rare original copy available for photographing.

Manufactured in the United States of America
Dover Publications, Inc., 31 East 2nd Street, Mineola, N.Y. 11501

Library of Congress Cataloging-in-Publication Data

Ecke, Gustav.
  Chinese domestic furniture in photographs and measured drawings.

  Reprint. Originally published: Chinese domestic furniture. Peking : Editions Henri Vetch, 1944.
  Bibliography : p.
  1. Furniture—China—History—Ming-ch'ing dynasties, 1368-1912. 2. Rosewood Furniture—China. I. Title.
NK2669.E34   1986   749.2951   86-6355
ISBN 0-486-25171-3

CONTENTS

	PAGE
Original Chinese title	VI
Publisher's Note, 1986	VII
Acknowledgments	VIII
List of Plates [general groupings]	X
Introduction	XIII
PRELIMINARY	XIII
THE BOX CONSTRUCTION AND ITS PLATFORM DERIVATIVES	XV
THE YOKE RACK AND KINDRED PLATFORM DEVICES	XXII
TRESTLE COMBINATIONS	XXV
THE SEAT	XXVI
SPLAY LEG CABINETS AND RELATED DESIGNS	XXX
SQUARE CASES	XXXI
CABINET WOODS	XXXIII
METAL MOUNTS	XXXVIII
CRAFTSMANSHIP—ORNAMENT—DATING	XL
CABINET MAKING AFTER YÜAN—RISE AND DECLINE	XLIII
CONCLUSION	XLIV
Bibliography	XLVII
Note [on furniture terminology]	LIII
List of Pieces [detailed descriptions]	LV
Original Chinese colophon	LX

PLATES 1 THROUGH 161

艾克 撰著

中國花梨家具圖考

楊宗翰署耑

Original Chinese title

PUBLISHER'S NOTE

The present edition of this rare classic is unabridged, but a number of technical alterations have been undertaken to make it both more convenient to the reader and decidedly more affordable than it was in its original format.

The original edition of 1944 was issued in a heavy cardboard portfolio. Contained inside were: (**1**) an unbound letterpress brochure, 9⅞″ × 12⅞″, including (in this order) a part title to the Introduction (omitted here); the dedication (transferred to the copyright page of this Dover edition); a title page and copyright page (replaced here by Dover's own); a table of contents that listed only the material in the brochure (and not the entire publication) and made no use of page numbers (Dover's new table of contents corrects both deficiencies); the Acknowledgments, the List of Plates and the line illustration preceding the Introduction (all on unnumbered pages); the Introduction (on pages numbered [1]–[34]); the Bibliography (on pages 35–[40]); and the Chinese-language colophon; and (**2**) a stack of (predominantly) individual leaves of heavy paper, 10⅜″ × 14¹⁵/₁₆″, including (in this order) another version of the title and copyright pages (omitted here); a part title to the Plates (replaced here by the new Dover version on page lxi); the calligraphed Chinese title page (which now faces this Publisher's Note); the Note (on furniture terminology; on pages numbered [v] and vi); the List of Pieces (on pages numbered [vii]–xi) [down to this point, all the leaves but the one numbered xi are printed on both sides, and the first two leaves (those preceding the Note) are joined in a little folder of four pages]; the 161 plates (on separate leaves, printed one side only, numbered 1–161; the large numbers above the rule are the plate numbers, the smaller numbers below the rule are those of the pieces of furniture); and another version of the Chinese-language colophon (omitted here).

Inasmuch as the Dover edition makes no distinction between these two chief groupings in terms of size, binding or type of paper, and in view of the fact that the only cross-references in the original text are to plate numbers, figure numbers and the numbers assigned to bibliographical entries (never to page numbers), it seemed best to consolidate all the material preceding the plates into a single Roman-numeral pagination, reserving Arabic numbers for the 161 plates. Running heads have been newly added. The Dover sequence and pagination are visible at a glance on the new contents page (v).

The Chinese title page (never transliterated or translated anywhere in the original edition) refers to "Aike"[1] (Ecke) as author (at the upper right) and to Yang Zonghan as calligrapher (at the lower left); in the center is the title, *Zhongguo huali jiaju tukao* (Pictorial Investigation of Chinese Rosewood[2] Furniture).

The Chinese colophon (now appearing on page lx; never translated in the original) reads as follows (in columns, right to left):

> Pictorial Investigation of Chinese Rosewood Furniture.
> Author: Aike [Ecke].
> Publisher: Weizhi [Vetch].
> Printer: (Collotypes) Caihua Yinshuaju [Colorful Splendor Printing Office], Peking;[3] Catholic[4] University Press, Peking; Imprimerie des Lazaristes,[5] Peking.
> Issued by: French Cultural Library, Peking.[6]
> October, 33rd year of the Chinese Republic [1944].

Finally, some further credits from one of the versions of the original copyright page: Drawings by Mr. Y. Yang [in characters: Yang Yue] and by the author. Inking by Mr. H. C. Chao [Zhao Xizhang]. Photographs taken at Hartung's Studio.

---

[1]In the present Publisher's Note, *pinyin* transcription is used.

[2]Strictly, *huali* (see page xxxv for a discussion of the terminology).

[3]The Chinese has "Beijing" although technically the city was called "Beiping" at the time.

[4]Literally, "Supporting Benevolence" or "Establishing Virtue." Presumably "Catholic" is correct here, since in one of the versions of the original copyright page the Catholic University Press is credited with the letterpress, together with the Imprimerie des Lazaristes.

[5]Literally, "Envoy Society [Congregation of the Mission] Printing Building."

[6]This is merely a literal translation, not necessarily the official designation. "Issued by" can also be rendered as "Wholesaler."

ACKNOWLEDGMENTS

In presenting a book on Chinese Furniture, I owe a number of acknowledgments to all who helped me with information and material. Twenty years ago, when I was travelling in Fukien, my eyes were first opened to the beauty of Chinese cabinet-work which is known so little in the West. Years later I was to meet again a friend of those early days, Professor Teng Yi-chih 鄧以蟄*, who furnished his home in Peking with rosewood pieces in the Ming style, and did not surrender to the taste of the day. This was the beginning of my renewed interest in the subject.*

In Mr. Yang Yüeh 楊耀 *I was fortunate to meet an artist and a draughtsman of genius to interpret, in line drawing, the spirit of Chinese furniture. To Dr. Henry S. Houghton, Director of the Peking Union Medical College, I am obliged for letting me see in MS his article on cabinet woods; to Mr. Paul P. Steintorf, American Trade Commissioner, for information on colonial woods; to Dr. H. H. Hu* 胡先驌, *Director of the Fan Memorial Institute of Biology, for the identification of Chinese woods; to Dr. H. Hattori, Director of the Tokugawa Institute for Biological Research, for the determination of a sample of Ming cabinet wood; to Dr. W. Bruell of the Catholic University, Peking, for his analysis of metal mounts.*

To all who allowed me to photograph and measure their furniture, with great inconvenience to themselves, I wish to express my gratitude. Their names appear in the List of Pieces. But I particularly have to mention Robert and William Drummond, whose active interest has enriched the present collection and the homes of many Peking residents.

In the correction of the English text I have been helped by the Rev. Professor William Fitzgibbon, S. V. D., while the references were checked by Mr. Achilles Fang, both of the Catholic University, Peking. I wish them to find here my sincere thanks. Professor Yang Tsung-han 楊宗翰 *graciously wrote in his own hand the Chinese title of the portfolio, thus giving distinction to the title page. To my publisher, Mr. Henri Vetch, I am much indebted for his unfailing help and inspiration in carrying through the work under trying and difficult conditions.*

But last and not least I remember with admiration the artisans of the Lu Pan Kuan. To them I owe a dedication of grateful esteem for lessons in practical skill and traditional workmanship. May their ancient and noble craft survive all perils of our mechanical civilisation.

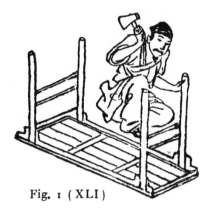

Fig. 1 (XLI)

GUSTAV ECKE

The Catholic University of Peking

June 1944

LIST OF PLATES

First Group (Plates 1 - 41): Square-legged Platforms
    Low Tables .... 2 - 5
    Braced-top Tables .... 6 right - 12
    Various Designs of High Tables .... 6 left, 13 - 16
    Forms of Feet .... 1,17 - 18
    Couches .... 19 - 28
    Bedsteads .... 29 - 39
    Foot-stools 40
    A Compound Design 41

Second Group (Plates 42 - 71): Round-legged Platforms
    Splay-leg Tables .... 42 - 55
    A Splay-leg Couch 56
    Bamboo Style Tables .... 43 top, 57 - 68
    Bracket Tables .... 69 - 71

Third Group (Plates 72-74): Special Forms of Tables
    A Semicircular Table; a Dressing Table 72
    Fancy Forms 73
    An Intermediate Form .... 74 top

Fourth Group (Plates 74-92): Boards with Trestle Supports
    Fixed Combinations .... 74 - 89
    Boards Supported on Separate Stands .... 90 - 91
    A Trestle Stand 92

Fifth Group (Plates 93 - 110): Various Forms of Seats
    The Construction of the Cane Seat 93
    Square-legged Stools 94
    Splay-leg Stools .... 95 - 96
    Bamboo Style Stools 97
    Back Chairs with Splat-back and Yoke .... 98 - 101
    An Armchair with Splat-back and Yoke 102
    Armchairs with Splat and Closed Back-frame ... 103 - 105
    Armchairs with Splat-back and Circular Rest ... 106 - 109
    Armchairs in the Bamboo Style 110

Sixth Group (Plates 111 - 122): Splay-leg Cabinets and Coffers
    Cabinets   111 - 117
    High-standing Coffers with Top Board   118 - 121
    A Low Cupboard with Drawers   122 bottom
Seventh Group (Plates 122 - 136): Square Cases
    A Low Cupboard with Drawers   122 - 124
    Compound Wardrobes   125 - 130
    Cabinets   131 - 133
    A Compound Cabinet   134
    Portable Cabinets   135 - 136
Eighth Group (Plates 137 - 151): Stands
    Occasional Stands (Circular)   137 - 141
    Lantern-stands   142
    Wash-stands   143 - 145
    Clothes-racks   146 - 147
    Carvings   148 - 151
Ninth Group (Plates 152 - 155): Joinery
    Joints 1 - 9   152
    Joints 10 - 17   153
    Joints 18 - 28   154
    Joints 29 - 34   155
Tenth Group (Plates 156 - 160): Metal Mounts
    Hinges   156
    Padlock Plates   157 - 158
    Pulls and Handles   159 - 160
Appendix Plate   161
    Ancestral Hall with Tablets and Portraits of the Chu Family at
    Chüanchow, Fukien; Sixteenth Century. (Note panel cutouts, lattice-
    work and furniture of simple domestic taste; author's photo, 1927).

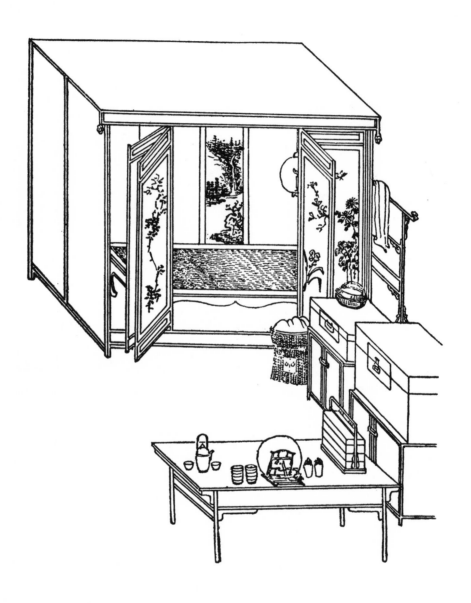

INTRODUCTION

La simplicité allant jusqu'à une sobriété sévère, la robustesse et la franchise des formes, livrant à même la qualité intrinsèque de la matière, annoncent les vertus éternelles de l'esthétique d'Extrême-Orient.

RENÉ GROUSSET, on Kansu Neolithic Pottery (XVI).

PRELIMINARY

Chinese furniture has retained its architectural character and the imprint of pristine dignity throughout changes of taste, unto the days of a dying tradition. Subordinate to the symmetry of the Chinese Hall (Fig. 2) it discloses methods which are likely to have arisen in the very beginning of Chinese culture (VIII, XXVIII). *

While this holds true even for elaborately carved and lacquered work (VI, XXXIII), it is particularly evident in plain hardwood pieces with their emphasis on structure. The latter have provided our examples. In our choice we have been guided by the Creative Spirit of the Chinese, wherever it reveals itself in the wood and in the interpretation of traditional patterns. Reserved in ornament and free from pretence, the rational features of Chinese domestic furniture more openly bring forth the vigour of the type and its adequacy (Frontispiece). The purity, the plastic strength, and the flawless polish of these pieces constitute their chief aesthetic appeal.

Such qualities will arouse the interest of the Western decorator who is ready to accept the merits of Queen Anne and similar tectonic design. In functional joinery the Craftsman of Soochow manifests his respect for the spirit of the wood and his command of line, curve and cubic proportion. Here are found the rules of Chinese cabinet-making which, in the early eighteenth century, became the ideal of the English ebonist. He learned and borrowed from China.

Documents for a history of Chinese furniture are numerous. In addition to literary references we have pictographs of Shang writing (pre-twelfth century B. C.); Shang and Chou bronzes (pre-third century B. C.);

* Throughout the text, Roman numerals in brackets refer to the Bibliography.

fragments of actual furniture from Han sites (third century B. C. to third century A. D.); excavations in Central Asia and the valley of the Yellow River; stands of Early Buddhist statuary; stone carvings and pictures from the Han Dynasty down to Castiglione and the end of the Empire; above all, however, the magnificent T'ang articles of furniture preserved in the Shosoin, the Treasure House at Nara (seventh and eighth centuries A. D.). But throughout the basic forms vary little. In the following pages their origin and development will be briefly touched upon.

Fig. 2 (XXVII)

THE BOX CONSTRUCTION AND ITS PLATFORM DERIVATIVES

The period of artless makeshifts ended in China long before the Culture of Anyang. From Shang scripts and from contemporary bronzes we conclude that the quality of early Chinese woodwork was not inferior to the perfection of bronze-casting, and that it had an even more ancient tradition. In fact, we have every reason to believe, that the two principal modes of joinery, as they survive today, were in the Shang period fully developed.

The Tuan-fang bronze tray (Fig. 3), from about 1300 to 1000 B. C., ranks as the foremost example of a platform construction with the box design, one of the two primary patterns for the construction of Chinese furniture. The bronze appears to be a metal translation of a wooden contrivance. The supporting frames enclose four panels on the long, and two on the short sides. Each panel has two rectangular ornamental openings and a decoration in relief that may correspond to painted designs. In this model the kind of jointing is not clear. A bronze of the Middle Chou period, however, imitates panel doors with frames (XXIII). These suggest the tongue and groove device, the mitre, and the dovetailed clamp of the panel so typical of Chinese joinery (joints 1, 1ª, 11ª, Pls. 152, 153). Considering the efficiency of the Shang bronze worker, one might assume that the Chinese joiner was very early acquainted with the technique of the mitred frame and with its aesthetic value (XIV).

This box-like structure can be imagined in varying sizes, as a low table, a seat, and as a large platform in the middle of the reception hall. The frame and panel construction of the dais in Fig.2, and its ritual position, have survived throughout three milleniums until the end of the Ch'ing Dynasty.

Two thousand years after the Tuan-fang tray the construction of the movable platform has not yet changed. Fig.4 is a reconstruction in the T'ang style and shows this clearly. Yet the pattern of the ornamental cutouts is an innovation probably developed during the Han period and the following centuries. The cusped and ogeed arch is known through many examples, particulary from the T'ang Dynasty. The form illustrated in Fig.4 is one among several varieties. Occasionally the panel is without the bottom part, and the upright sections finish on the sill in footlike enlargements. Even further simplifications are met with in T'ang and earlier examples: such as the omission of the bottom frame, a fusion of the quoin supports, and so on (Fig.10); but they are not the rule. For centuries to follow, the complete biparted frame and panel construction of the carcase remains the standard.

About the end of the ninth century new forms are developed, and with them new modifications of the cusped arch, while the ogee is not forgotten. The clear separation of frame and panel is preserved at least in principle. The lower portion of the panel, however, disappears for good; and the upper part becomes a kind of indented apron-like notch-board.

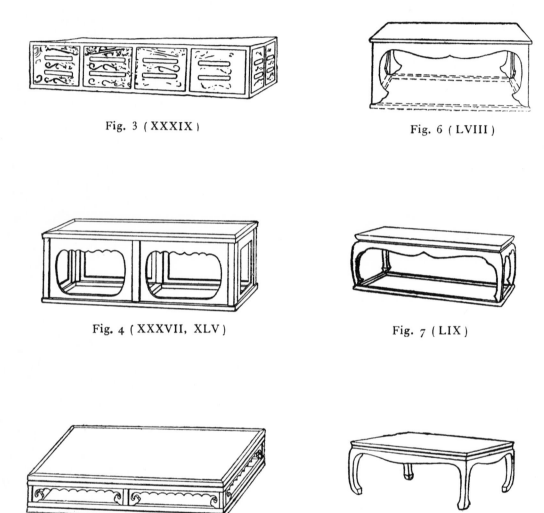

Fig. 3 (XXXIX)

Fig. 6 (LVIII)

Fig. 4 (XXXVII, XLV)

Fig. 7 (LIX)

Fig. 5 (XXXVIII)

Fig. 8 (Pl. 2)

The footlike endings of the panel uprights are fashioned into far-projecting, crocketed, and pointed scrolls. Fig. 5 shows a couch in this style. The drawing is from a copy attributed to the Sung Emperor Hui-tsung, and made after an earlier original, perhaps of the tenth century. The elaborate design of this structure is of mongrel character. It represents a transition in the development towards a later manner of movable platform.

The first indication of this final change appears in the type of Fig. 6. Here the bipartition definitely has been given up, and the carcase unified through a fusion of the frame with the panels. The corner uprights consist of narrow slats, the remnants of the former panel ends, jointed at a right angle. The outer edge preserves the line of the former separate stiles and thus is straight. The inner borders of the slats retain the curving of the panel cutouts; and the lower edge of the apron has the form of a cusped arch with lateral ogees which swing into the curves of the supporting slats. Above the bottom frame these quoin slats flare into wing-like scrolls that are boldly curved and pointed. This style seems to have flourished in the thirteenth and fourteenth centuries (cf. the footstool of Fig. 24); in the making of lacquered furniture as also in some forms of carved stands for bibelots and bronzes it has continued to the present day.

The only survival of the former bipartition at this stage of development is the bottom frame. It remains important for reasons of structure and protection. The strength of the carcase depends on it more than ever, and it keeps the supports from the moisture of the flagstones. The bottom frame was still in use at the beginning of the fifteenth century; the quoin slats had by that time solidified into square legs. Only few pieces of this kind remain complete in their original condition, since the bottom frame is the first part of the structure to suffer or to be lost.

The quoin device of a stand of early character (Piece 71, Pl. 92) has an inner frame that is a remnant of the separate panel. The outer, supporting frame slats (cf. Fig. 4) of the original construction are here solidified into square legs. It is probable that such constructions were used during the transition time to strengthen the carcase of larger platforms (cf. Fig. 5).

Fig. 7, a Japanese piece of early Ming design, illustrates the final evolution of the solid legs. While the bottom frame is retained, the actual platform structure is now further unified and strengthened through a fusion of the two quoin slats into solid square legs. The most conspicuous feature of this solidification is the survival in the feet of the pointed panel scroll. The result is what the Chinese cabinet makers call *ma-t'i* 馬蹄, a 'horse-hoof' (Pl. 1), which has remained a peculiar characteristic of the square leg ever since the beginning of the Ming period, but disappears as a weak scroll with the decay of artistic taste (Piece 19, Pl. 25). Our examples 27 and 28 (Pl. 40), or 72 and 73 (Pl. 94) illustrate the original vigour of the horse-hoof foot, and what had become of it towards the end of the eighteenth century. The scroll in the style of Piece 19 (cf. XLVII, passim) had almost replaced by that time the old horse-hoof. A sad example is seen in Piece 7 (Pl. 8). Formerly a magnificent table, it has recently lost about

Fig. 9 (XLIII)

40 cm from its height. To the original foot which was like the one shown in Piece 10 (Pl. 11), the dealer substituted a combination of weakly carved bits of wood glued to the mutilated legs. Examples 14ᵃ and 14 (Pl.17), show the open foot form contrasted with the solid horse-hoof, and once more suggest the transition from jointed slats to square legs. Pieces 6, 3ᵃ and 110 (Pls. 18, 137) give diverse forms of this prototype of the Western club-foot.

Interesting to note in these formal developments is the growth and final triumph of the curvilinear principle. It originated with the sweeping bends of the panel cutouts (Figs. 4 - 6) and ends up by dominating the outlines of the entire carcase (Figs. 7,8). With the evolution of the horse-hoof leg the external edges of the quoins, originally straight in accordance with the frame and panel device (Figs. 3-6), become curved by assimilation with the internal edge (Piece 4, Pl. 5). This is at the very least true of the edges of the feet. It is difficult to decide if, in the choice of the name 'hoof', there survives the remembrance of a leg motif common in the Han style (cf. L, Pl. 70; LIV, Pls. 48-59; LIII, vol. IX, Pl. 50, the latter a T'ang adaptation), and which had Central Asian and Hellenistic-Roman affinities (Fig. 9). Its cabriole curve even may be related to the form of the Li vessel that can claim a neolithic ancestry. The ancient Western prototype, fused with later Chinese forms, inspired the 'pied-de-biche', the cabriole curves of which engaged Hogarth's aesthetic speculation. The legs of pieces 3 and 3ᵃ (Pls. 3, 18) are in their compressed proportions close to the Han motif of Fig. 9. In Japanese tables slender cabriole legs of Sung or earlier inspiration have been preserved (LI, Pl. 90). Piece 111 (Pl. 139), of about 1600 A. D., shows a similar slender leg with a foot form that has been taken over almost exactly in the West by Boulle and other masters of his day.

But the classic Chinese solution of the curvilinear problem is found in Piece 110 (Pl. 137), perhaps a fifteenth century design. This tripod stand, unified through its circular plan, has been reduced to the bare essentials of construction. The slender legs have an elongated S-form and flare into weighty club-feet, which are tenoned into the bottom frame (Pl. 138). Continuous cabriole and ogee curves, together with the points of the apron cusps endow its form with rhythmic grace and vigour. The elastic freedom and the purity of this lotus-like creation has perhaps not been surpassed in China, and certainly not in the West where the bronze stand from Pompeii (XIII, Fig. 25; cf. also Fig. 24) represents the height of perfection.

We now revert to the rectangular plan, the final form of the platform construction. Even here the bottom frame is not quite abandoned. It survives especially in small, in ornamental pieces, or where stability makes it indispensable (Piece 29, Pl. 41). Tables and couches, however, are constructed more and more without this last remainder of the bipartite substructure. This requires further simplification and, from the craftsman, greater skill. Pieces 1 and 15 (Pls. 2, 19) indicate what may be achieved. A new and independant version of the platform has been evolved which one would associate with the Tuan-fang tray only by tracing its pedigree (Figs. 3-8).

The elegance of couch table 1 is obvious. The most has been made of the possibilities contained in the tensile quality of the red sandalwood; for its curves and proportions could not be bettered. The bend of the legs, the paw-like thrust of the feet, the bulge of the outline, carry the mirror-like plane of the top from which they are separated by a deep hollow. The design of this table reveals a mature sense of harmony and tension not even foreshadowed in the archaic box with its frame and panel carcase (Fig. 3).

Couch 15 (cf. Frontispiece), however, ought to be compared with its relative, the ceremonial dais reproduced in Fig. 2. This platform has remained in principle part of the house construction, preserving the original frame and panel device unaltered; the couch, after evolving over twenty-five centuries, has become in itself a piece of architecture.

We reproduce the foot of this structure in actual size on Pl. 1. It shows how the peculiar essence of the huali rosewood, its grain and its fibric energy, harmonise with contour and volume in the very function of the solid foot.

The perfection of this plain couch, self-supporting and self-sufficient, makes one regret that back- and arm-rests ever should have been introduced. Yet the attempt to combine the Chinese platform with an imported railing may, after a period of experimentation (Fig. 24), lead to harmonious results (Piece 16, Pl. 20). For the design of chairs similar problems were met with and successfully solved (IX, passim).

In couch railings and in the lattice-work of testered bedsteads, motifs were employed which are known to the student of Chinese architecture. Square, swastika and other simple patterns are seen in pieces which may be early Ming. They are included in Professor D. S. Dye's *Grammar of Lattice Work* (VII). The lattice bars of huali wood are usually slightly fluted with the exception of the sides that face the wall. For wood of a different character a convex moulding may be preferred (Piece 20,

Pl. 26). Plates 37, 38 and Joint 12 on Pl.153 show the kind of mortising commonly used.

A comparison of two couches with board railings again helps to throw light on the growth and change of taste. Piece 21 (Pl. 27) shows a prevalence of the straight line along with features that seem to indicate an early Ming date (cf. Piece 6). Its austere strength is enhanced through the inner splay of the legs. With its large-figured single-board rests, its arched metal mounts, and flawless linear proportions, this couch is one of the most representative examples of patrician household furniture.

Couch 22 (Pl. 28) by itself is also quite an impressive piece. But, when compared with the other couch, its massive design looks heavy, the broken horizontals lack clarity, and the cumbrous feet fail to achieve the effect of the monumental. The double hollow between substructure and seat frame connects the style of this couch with that of stool 73 (Pl. 94); the feet and moulding, with the stand of ice-box 29 (Pl. 41). Stand 5 (Pl. 6) belongs to the same group of late pieces. They represent a Ch'ienlung or Chiach'ing style, which continued down to the end of the Empire. Thus between the two couches, 21 and 22, it would be reasonable to assume a difference of three or four hundred years in age.

The early illustration of a testered bedstead (fourth century A. D.), included in the London copy of Ku K'ai-chih's Admonitions, has been often reproduced (LIV, Fig. 30). Other examples are preserved among the Tun-huang paintings. Our Fig.10 shows a less known example from a stone carving of Vimalakirti in the style of the Six Dynasties (sixth century A. D.). It is a kind of four-poster bed, naturally with separate construction of bed and canopy. In its simplified design the bed of the Ming period (Piece 23, Pl. 29) seems to be anticipated. The bedstead reproduced as Piece 26 (Pl. 39) again displays the simple magnificence of early huali furniture. It is a veritable alcove architecture.

With the introduction of Buddhism, the Chinese gradually got accustomed to the Western sitting posture. While the type of the low table survives from the days of squatting and cross-legging, there now originates a new kind of table resembling in form and usage the European form. Pictorial evidence proves that, into the days of the Sung and Yüan periods, the bottom frame was employed also with these high structures. An extant example, probably an early Ming piece, is stand 6. It is an occasional table with the bottom frame complete.

Its intricate make is of Chinese inspiration. The slight splay of the legs is brought out through a hardly perceptible downward contraction (Pl.7). The splay is stayed by the bottom frame, into which the club-feet are

Fig. 10 (XV)

locked by means of a subtle device (Joint 20^a, Pl. 154). But it is the mode of coupling the legs with the table top that inaugurates a new method of construction. Early illustrations show how the uprights of the side-pieces are bent at the top to support the table. An example of this is Fig.17, taken from a T'ang picture; it reproduces a *chi* 几 table with remarkable accuracy. Whether, or not, tables with these bent uprights still existed in Yüan and Ming times, we do not know. It rather looks as if this kind of support had been adapted to the new braced-top invention. If so, the oblique braces (Piece 7, Pl.8) would derive from the earlier side brackets, (Fig.17). Turned into such braces, they were grappled and doweled to the clamps of the table top (Joint 18^a, Pl. 154) exactly as in z of Fig. 17. But instead of directly conveying the pressure to the bottom sill, they transmit it, below the shoulders, to the legs, into which they are wedged and tenoned (joints 19, 19^a, Pl. 154). They thus effectively relieve the complicated shoulder joints (Joint 3, Pl. 152). In case of square, or nearly square tables, as in the two pieces 6 and 7, whenever the four braces are long enough to meet in the middle of a central clamp, a hanging cover is employed (Pls. 7, 8; joints 18, 18^a, Pl. 154). This offers additional security; at the same time it conceals the grapnels of the central junction and thus harmonises the design (Pl. 8, bottom), which now recalls that of centralised timber ceilings (XXVI). The result of connecting the braced top with a bottom frame is a compound carcase of dynamic stability, a construction that has remained unique in the making of furniture. Examples 8 to 11 (Pls.9-12) show larger pieces without bottom frames; examples 12 and 13 (Pls. 13, 14), a modified lateral bracing.

A curious remnant of the bottom frame is the tenon-like termination of the club-foot occasionally employed with low tables, to insure a firm hold of the leg in the mattress of the couch (Piece 3^a, Pl.18).

Attempts to do without the securing bottom frame introduced the top-tie of timber architecture. We reproduce bench-table 4 (Pl. 5) to represent an early example. For small rectangular stands, a subsequent innovation raised the bottom frame above the feet and changed it into a system of stretchers, as shown in 5 and 70 of Pls. 6 and 91. We have put stand 5 by the side of the braced-top stand on the same plate, in order to let a powerful Ming piece appear next to a later adaptation.

For the sake of clarity and reserve all securing devices were occasionally abandoned. Table 14 (Pl. 15) with its high and slender legs is a distinguished example of this; and, just as a psaltery table, perhaps firm enough. The plainness observed in this design reminds us again of the primitive Tuan-fang bronze stand, but the platform is now elevated and, after a hundred generations, transformed through a final advance in taste.

This over-simplified construction, however, does not inspire confidence. Such design rather than the ancient frame and panel tray (Fig.3) would deserve to be cast in metal.

THE YOKE RACK AND KINDRED PLATFORM DEVICES

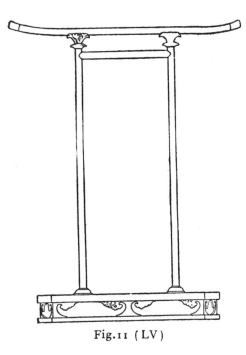

Fig.11 (LV)

The rack, as shown in Fig. 11, represents the primary unit of the Chinese post and rail design. Usually set at a splay, it is the fundamental of the architectural timber frame and of the most elementary kinds of movable furniture. Down to the present day their structural forms have preserved an archaic appearance unaltered. A Shang pictograph (Fig. 12) shows, naturally without yoke and splay, a gate-like arrow rack that might have been made in the nineteenth century. A T'ang clothes rack in the Shosoin (Fig. 11; cf. Frontispiece, and pieces 121, 122, Pls. 146, 147) is as near to a modern Chinese shan-lan 欄柵 gate or to a Japanese torii (IX, p. 40) as to splay-legged table 30 (Fig.14) of early Ming design. Couch-like bench 42 (Pl.56), with its rounded legs firmly planted on the ground, seems to be the direct and almost unaltered offspring of the ancient ch'uang 牀, as represented in the Shang pictograph. And not less archaic are the splay-leg cabinets that will be discussed lower down.

The prominent feature of all these rack designs is the capping. To form the substructure of a table or a bench, the rack is duplicated and splayed in both directions; the two racks are united by ties, while their yokes

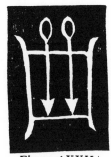

Fig.12 (XXII)

serve as longitudinal frame pieces to the top. An apron board, of architectural origin, is added (joints 7, 8, Pl. 152).

The longitudinal rail may pierce through the posts (Fig. 14) or simply be mortised into them. In the construction of most splay-leg tables these rails are omitted. Where they appear, they indicate an earlier version of the design, which more closely follows the architectural. The posts may undergo formal development, and lose their roundness. But the chief characteristics of the design remain: the splay of the legs for stability; the yoke; and the connective ties. A comparison of pieces 6 (Fig.13) and 30 (Fig.14) shows the difference between the two principal modes of construction, the box carcase with its bottom frame, and the yoke table standing free on its splayed legs.

The character of the post and rail construction, however standardised, offered opportunities of variation not less interesting than the curvilinear development of the box design. Viewing pieces 30 and 37 (Pls. 42, 48, 49) side by side, one understands the degree of grace which an archaic model may achieve within its structural limits. Pieces 36 and 40 (Pls. 46, 47, 51 - 53) are both classical, the one in tectonic simplicity and harmony, the other in the greatness of a form, that is enlivened by the rhythm and swell of outline and the subtleness of subdivision.

Fig. 13 (Pl. 6)

Fig. 14 (Pl. 42)

Perhaps the most impressive example in this group of splay-legged platforms is table 41 (Pl. 55). Its strength in both material and composition is uncommon. Making use of the conventional style, and in harmony with the nature of the wood (Pl. 54), the forms of this structure are replete with grandeur. Not often the function of load and stay in furniture design is as clearly visible as in the splay of these table legs; their feet flare as if forced outwards by overpowering pressure (cf. Pl. 79). The severity of this pattern is relieved by an exquisite poise of proportion.

To indicate once more the ancient lineage of the yoke construction, the sketch of a small splay-leg bronze table of the third century B. C. is added here in Fig. 15. With a concave top board, its form is akin to that

Fig. 15 (XLVIII)

of small squatting benches or head-rests still used in China to-day.

Closely connected with the post and rail contrivance, and probably just as ancient, is the bamboo style. Its architectural affinities are less striking. Examples 31 and 46, put together on Pl. 43, illustrate both kinship and difference. The outstanding feature of the bamboo style is a cornice evenly projecting, as contrasted with the lateral overhang of the board-ends. Piece 46 (Pl. 43, top) imitates, in hardwood, a bamboo structure. So does hardwood table 44 (Pl. 58) which reproduces another related form. The bamboo designs represented in naturalistic faithfulness by examples 46 and 44 have both contributed some typical forms of tables. Examples 47, 48 and 49 (Pls. 63, 64, 65 top), deriving from a prototype shown in Example 46, have a more domestic, if not commonplace, character. Example 44, however, represents a pattern that has inspired works of original stamp. In its derivatives, the reeded cornice is replaced by forms of an entablature similar to that of tables descending from the box design, though here less standardised. Table 45, in moulding and composition, still follows the bamboo prototype, but in a free and independent manner (Pls. 59-62). Example 51 adopts the square legs from the box-derived platform and replaces the brackets by latticed spandrels (Pl. 67). The straight line dominates throughout (Pl. 68); the carcase is highly unified but, at the same time, delicately moulded and subdivided. The hollowing of stiles, rails, and bars, the fluted chamfers of the edges, bring about the changing contrasts of light and shade that animate the geometrical beauty of this unique creation (Pl. 66; cf. Pl. 65, bottom and Pls. 127, 132).

Tables 45 and 51 reveal the reserve of the Chinese designer, who adjusted his individual taste to a conventional conception, avoiding the barrenness of austerity just as much as the danger of baroque decay.

The more traditional tables, on the other hand, may possess simple merits of their own. Pieces 52, 53 and 54 (Pls. 69-71) are of a type familiar to those who have travelled up-country. With their rounded legs, they belong to the post and rail group, while other characteristics connect them to the yoke and the bamboo groups. Peculiar to this type are the oblique corner brackets that help to support the evenly projecting cornice. A structural apron is added; and to this, a rigid, strongly moulded rail, which accompanies and enhances the broken contours of the apron. Plate 70 shows the vigour of such an archaic construction.

TRESTLE COMBINATIONS

This section comprises three kinds of tables. The ancestry of the first group is indicated in the Shang pictograph of the modern character *chi* 几. It suggests the arm-support for a reclining person; and at the same time, a low table placed on the ground or on the couch. The small bronze table of Fig. 16, of Shang or early Chou origin, represents the ancient construction: a board laid on plain side pieces. The same combination 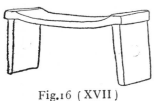 continued to be used through the milleniums. A late adaptation, but still in the Ming style, is shown in a portrait by Yü Chih-ting (about 1700), where a scholar is seen cross-legged on a mat with the chi table (LII) next to him. Raised to sitting height,

Fig.16 (XVII)

without projections of board ends and sills, this trestle table is used as a psaltery stand (Piece 60, Pl. 75). The high side pieces are spandrelled (Pl. 76); the scrolls, reeds and beads are typical of an early reticent design (Pls. 77, 78).

The second group, comprising pieces 61 to 68, may derive from a primitive prototype still in common use: it is the combination of splay-leg trestle benches (cf. Fig. 15) with a detachable top board. For the fixed structure, the yoke table seems to have been used as the pattern. The board-ends project yoke-like, but the side pieces tend to be perpendicular, though a slight splay of aesthetic value is occasionally retained (Pl. 85). Among the various trestles illustrated, some have remarkable decorative motifs, such as feet with a structural outward flare (Pl. 79), a boldly sculptured openwork (Pl. 82), and specimens of beautiful panel tracery (Pl. 81).

A noteworthy motif is the up-turned board end (Pl. 79, right top) employed, in an almost identical form, on a Han desk tray (L, Pl. 56) excavated in Korea (Pl. 79, left top) and in a T'ang painting (Fig. 17). These up-turned edges are found both on splay-leg tables and on the top boards of standing coffers (Joint 9, Pl. 152). They have aesthetic as well as practical value.

These side boards, with and without the up-turned edges, are used still today in many households. A remarkable specimen with a plain top board, probably a Ch'ienlung design, is Piece 68 (Pl. 89), veneered with broad sheets of grayish bamboo and enriched with hungmu beads. We shall come back to this table later.

Another ancestor of this side board may be seen in an ancient trestle table known to have been used in China from Han (LIV, Pls, 70-73,

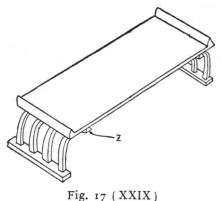

Fig. 17 (XXIX)

Figs. 27-29; L, Pl. 71) to T'ang times (Fig. 17), and, in a simplified form with straight spindles, as late as the Sung. In this latter form, as also with slightly curved spindles, the table survives in Japan to the present day.

The characteristic bracket-like uprights in the side pieces of the early type have already been discussed. Round or angular, they are tenoned into the sill and grappled to the clamps of the top board (z, Fig. 17). Example 59 (Pl. 74), with open, frame-like side pieces, may be a simplification of the archaic prototype, while the proportions and the up-turned edges of Piece 58 (Pl. 74, top) may likewise derive from the now obsolete Chinese design.

Complete trestle tables with detachable top boards are quite rare (pieces 69, 70, Pls. 90, 91). These tops require a faultless and seasoned wood, as neither cleat nor clamp protect them from warping. Their solid boards were a splendid treasure-trove which, with the exhaustion of old stocks, has been continually plundered for the making of new furniture.

Piece 71 (Pl. 92.) is a single trestle support, most likely an early Ming example. The type also serves as an occasional table. The timeless beauty of this square stand is at once apparent. Along with the circular stands 110, 112, and 120 (Pls. 137, 141, 145), it proves the perfection the Chinese ebonist was able to achieve in both rectangular and curvilinear composition. A strictly radial symmetry is, as in architecture, the pre-requisite condition of such absolute design.

THE SEAT

Stools 72, 73 (Pl. 94), 74, 75 (Pl. 95), 76, 77 (Pl. 97), affiliated, respectively, with the frame and panel, the post and rail, and the bamboo constructions, represent the three seat designs that are likely to have come down from the earliest days of Chinese joinery.

Square, and originally large in size, as on the T'ang image of Amoghavajra attributed to Li Chen (XVIII), they served as platforms for single persons in a kneeling or cross-legged posture. When, in the course of the first Buddhist centuries, the Western mode of sitting became popular, a back-rest with or without side-arms combined with the traditional Chinese structures. With the wholesale adaptation of Indo-Central Asian back- and arm-chairs to the Chinese architectural style (IX, p. 40 sqq.)

the plain Chinese chair developed. It employed and fused the three stool forms mentioned above.

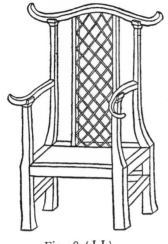

Fig. 18 (LI)

Fig. 19 (XLIV)

There seem to have existed, from the beginning, two principally different kinds of adaptation. The one type (Fig. 18) used, with architectural chapiters, a chair with upright back frame designed after the conventional Chinese yoke rack pattern which is akin to the Indian yoke design (Fig. 11). The other adapted to Chinese taste (Fig. 19) the Indian, or Indo-Central Asian, chair with circular rest.

A peculiar characteristic of the adapted Chinese chair is the splat which appears already fully developed in the earliest extant example (Fig. 20), a Sung piece of about 1100 A. D. (cf. IX, note 25). Its structural meaning is obvious. It replaces the uncomfortable rail of the original yoke frame which, moreover, here insufficiently secures. The first step towards inventing the vertical stripe of wood in the centre of the back-rest may be seen in the two parallel uprights connecting crest and seat frame in the early type of Fig. 18. These uprights are here fitted with an elastic caning of which only the basic webbing (cf. Pl. 93, top) is indicated. Thus, within the yoke rack of the new chair back, the horizontal rail was replaced by a vertical caned frame; and this, finally, by the solid back splat.

Fig. 20 (IX)

As early as the period of Philip II of Spain, an isolated Chinese folding chair, with splat-back and yoke, found its way to the West (Fig. 21). It was at the time not imitated. But more than a hundred years later the solid splat came into fashion as a dominating motif of the European chair. The formal development of the European splat motif and its later elaboration are familiar to the student of art history. In most cases in China the splat preserved its plain frontal silhouette, but obtained aesthetic significance from the lateral sinuous curving (Pls. 99, 101, 108), from the colour and grain of the wood (Piece 80, Pl. 102). Occasionally a medallion-like opening at the top with a lower narrow cutout, or an ornamental burl-wood panel, adorns the splat without changing its frontal outline (Piece 79, Pl. 100). Also a carved cartouche may be introduced into the top; this is enhanced by ogeed lateral projections, the only enrichment of the frontal silhouette ever employed in the Chinese splat motif (Piece 87, Pl. 107, cf. Fig. 21).

Fig. 21
(XIII)

Piece 78 represents a modest though typical example of the back chair with splat-back and yoke (Pls. 98, 99). It is of the ordinary domestic type which continued to be made, with slight modifications, until our time. The crest, in the form of two flat S-curves and with an emphasis on the caved neck-rest, resembles a porter's yoke. Curved uprights cut out of the solid wood like the splat, flank the latter and follow or complement its curve. Additional rails with two breaks appear on the three principal sides below the seat. These rails are vertically connected with the top rails by short propping uprights. The seat frame is supported at the back by a plain bracketed apron. The front rung is flattened into a foot-rest and, like the lateral stretchers, secured by a notch-board. The height of this seat, as that of most Chinese chairs and couches, which vary from about 48 to 52 cm., suggests the use of separate foot-stools. The latter keep the feet from the damp pavement (Figs. 2, 24; Pl. 40).

The construction seen in the cane seat is the same in all caned couches, beds, stools, benches, and chairs described here, though in only a few cases the original caning is preserved. The seat frame of stool 77 was photographed during two successive stages of a reparation. The pictures reproduced on Pl. 93 together with the details of joints 26 and 27 (Pl. 154) helps to interpret our measured drawings of caned seats.

Dr. R. P. Hommel, in his *China at Work* (XX, p. 312), describes the basic webbing as a « surface of interwoven chamaerops cords, fastened to the edges of the wooden frame, in the same way as our cane chair seats are attached in a row of holes along the edges ». In the case of more refined seat constructions a cane seat, woven in patterns familiar from Western chairs, is laid upon the webbing. The ends of both cane and webbing are passed through the same holes (T) and tied on the underside of the frame. A thin strip frame (L) is then applied to cover the holes and is fastened with dowel pins (U). Strong ties (V), caved or bent, and tenoned into the seat frame, secure the whole contrivance which proves to be as comfortable and firm as that of the Western cane seat. The question whether, or not, Spanish and Dutch traders brought the Chinese caning technique to Europe remains to be studied.

Back chair 79 is related to psaltery table 60, not only in the lustre of the golden-yellow rosewood, but in the restrained style that shows something of the character of a bygone Chinese house interior. Well might the two pieces be imagined as part of the scholar's home suggested by Yü Chih-ting (LII). Beardsley and Morris, even more than Shareton, would have delighted in such simplified design. Armchair 81 (Pl. 103), reduced to mere proportions, is a piece of equal charm. It represents another very common sort of domestic chair. Its closed back-frame has been the model for the hoop of the Western splat-back chair (pieces 82-84, Pls. 104, 105).

From the kind of sturdy creation illustrated as Fig. 19—made by a carpenter rather than by a joiner—the circular rest gradually evolved lighter and more inspired forms. In the beginning of the Ming Dynasty, or even earlier, it may have attained its ultimate harmony of composition. The combination of circular back- and arm-rails, united by cogged scarf joints (22, 22^a, 22^b, Pl. 154), results in a continuous bow that usually ends in outward turning curves and scrolls. To replace the discarded neck-rest (Fig. 19), the bow is now sloped. It is supported by the back legs produced above the seat frame, by separate uprights, and by the bracketed extensions of the front legs. Chair 87 (Pl. 107) with alternating straights and curves, with slanting, diverging, and converging lines held in the sweep of the bow, brings forth an effect of graceful dignity. The spandrels of the front legs are double scrolls, giving a gay appearance to an otherwise very stately settle.

The bamboo style chair, related to our examples 88,89 (Pl.110), has been discussed by Hommel (XX, p. 309). For the Western student the type is of interest, as it was made use of by Adam in furnishing a bedroom at Claydon House—the first instance of Chinese domestic furniture entering a European home (XXX).

Fig. 22 (X)

It is not improbable that the Shang pictograph of Fig. 22 represents the earliest high-standing cupboard, but without the splay and without the door wings; a sacrificial vessel rests on the bottom shelf. Siamese cabinet-makers, who adapted Chinese models, may have preserved an obsolete Chinese cupboard form; they employ ornamental extensions of the stiles, though not of the mullions, above the cupboard top (V). In China similar prolongations and ornamental cappings are found still today on the posts of ceremonial gates and shop fronts (XXV, Pl. 6). The extant type of the Chinese splay-leg cabinet does not possess these upward prolongations, but has a character not less archaic. Its simplicity and tectonic vigour make it a typical Chinese creation. The constructional method employed for the carcase (Pl. 115) resembles that of a splay-leg table. The lateral ties are discarded, and the sills, aproned. These aprons usually show the straight line seen in the splay-leg table, but the brackets occasionally have forms derived from the cutouts of the ancient frame and panel design (Pl. 113; cf. Pl. 11 and Figs. 6, 24). The door wings, as in architecture, swing on pivots provided by the prolongations of additional uprights (Pl. 116). Clustered stiles produce a particularly strong and vivid effect. (Pl. 113).

One of the outstanding examples among these cabinets, perfect in structural design and restrained composition, is Piece 90 (Pl. 111). The stilted feet give it unusual distinction; the large beautiful huali panels, a quiet charm hardly to be matched.

The splay-leg chest illustrated as Piece 97 (Pl. 118) is in reality a coffer on legs with top board. Its origin is unknown, but it might be connected with an ancient coffer-like receptacle, of which examples are preserved in the Shosoin (LIII, vol. IV, Pl. 26), and survive in Japanese temples as chests for Buddhist scriptures. This archaic structure represents a coffer hung up in a splay-leg stand. One only needs to add a top board with bracketed lateral projections, reduce the width of the body, and add surrounding rails, to arrive at something like the high-standing coffer of our two examples. The actual receptacle remains in all adaptations the sunken shelf (Pl. 119, cross-section). The drawers seem to be later additions to the original coffer type, turning to advantage the compartments of the railed carcase.

An all-round treatment of the standing coffer makes it probable that this type of furniture traditionally occupied a position in which the sides and the back were as much in evidence as the front. Similar splay-leg structures made of unfinished elmwood serve as meat-boards for Peking mutton butchers (XXV, Pl. 24, top). They fill exactly one half of the originally open shop front (cf. LVI), thus explaining the name «chest of the door-wing», *men-hu-ch'u* 門戶廚, which, however, is used now only for refined huali pieces. In most households a pair of these coffers used to be a portion of the bride's trousseau.

The front notch-board of these structures appears as a silhouetted apron, usually adorned with lateral scrolls flanking the traditional cusp and ogee pattern and a central scallop ornament (Pl. 120). The front panels of the drawers are enriched with a kindred glued frame; With their scrolled brackets they derive from the ornamental cutouts of the frame and panel platform. Connected with this splay-leg coffer is the splay-leg chest of drawers (Piece 99, Pl. 122, top), which is still today one of the most common kinds of domestic furniture.

SQUARE CASES

Low-standing cupboard 100 (Pl. 122-124) has a simplified carcase. Its rectangular body is that of a plain chest. The front surface of stiles, rails, and panels below the drawers, is cut flush; and the sunken panels of drawers, sides, and back do not interfere with the general cubic appearance.

The origin of this rectangular type is obvious. It derives from the primitive chest indicated in the Shang pictograph of character *fang* 匚. To protect the chest from the dampness of the ground it was kept on a stand as seen in Fig. 4. The Shosoin still preserves examples of this combination (LIII, vol. VII, Pls. 19-21). An upward development followed; the low chest changed into a standing case with doors as shown in an early T'ang example, likewise preserved in the Shosoin (Fig. 23). Similar cases with stands are still used in Korea to the present day. The next step was to fuse the stiles of the case with the stiles of the stand, and to extend them further

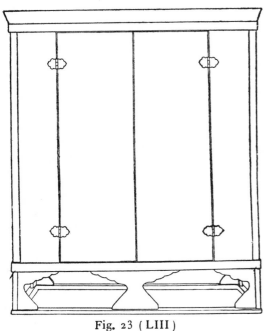

Fig. 23 (LIII)

into feet. The representative pieces of the resulting type retain in the framework traces of the original compound character in the two sills, indicated in the cross-section of Piece 103 as 'middle rail' and 'bottom rail' (Pl. 130). They are reminiscent of the original separation of case and stand (Fig. 23). The middle rail still suggests the bottom shelf of the primitive case; the bottom rail takes the place of the sill member of the stand; while the combined stiles of case and stand extend, as has been said, into the feet of the new creation.

Another proof of the original composite character of this case may be seen in the addition of plain top pieces, which form part of a compound wardrobe set (Pls. 125, 126). The stiles of these low top pieces may simply be extended into feet (Pl. 122), thus making it possible to convert the top chest into a low cupboard or chest of drawers. The body may be increased in height and become a cabinet (Pl. 131) and may be supplied again with a top chest of its own (Pl. 134). All these standing chests and cabinets, however, have now only one sill, the bottom rail, which is usually equipped with a notch-board.

The wardrobe sets of four have a monumental character; in graduated standard sizes they were part of every household, whether of the commoner or of the prince. Separated (Pl. 126), or side by side (Pl. 125), they occupy a permanent place of architectural import. They are the treasury of the family, and their huge padlocks (cf. XX, p. 295) add to their grandeur. In the Imperial Palace sets may still be seen along the walls in symmetrical disposition; the top pieces occasionally multiply so that, on the principal piece, three superimposed low chests are supported, which creates a truly majestic impression.

Wardrobe 103 (Pl. 127) is an example of particular interest. It shows how a plain chest composition may be embellished without endangering the restraint and the greatness of its cubic architecture. All uprights and rails, save those facing the wall, have flat hollows recalling the Gothic Linenfold; the edges finish in fluted chamfers. The panels, nine of them in the front, have middle fields formed by sunken rectangular borderstrips, with cusps in the four corners of each field. The plain rectangular hinges and padlock plates are adjusted to the profiles of the panel frames (Pl. 158, right top). Their smooth polish combines with the hollows of the frame pieces and the mouldings of the panels to produce a play of soft and shifting lights. The proportion of the two superimposed pieces, the subdivision of the front, and the boldly silhouetted apron boards add linear rhythm to the chestnut-coloured huali wood (Pl. 128). The interior arrangement, with its inner front, and open as well as concealed shelves and drawers (Pl. 129), is a marvel of intricate craftsmanship (Pl. 155). The general appearance of this set of four parts is at once simple and magnificent. It competes with the best Perpendicular Flemish pieces.

CABINET WOODS

«The climatic conditions in China... make it desirable for the people who can afford it, to have their furniture constructed from wood which can withstand... severe changes. We find therefore that a great variety of hard woods, partly of native growth, but more frequently imported from the tropical regions of South-Eastern Asia, are employed in constructing the furniture of the Chinese house» (Hommel, XX, pp. 244, 245).

In the market and in Chinese encyclopaedias, cabinet woods are known only by their trade names. It is difficult to arrive at the botanical names, especially so in the absence of a clear distinction between indigenous and imported varieties. Among modern scientists, both Chinese and Western, «no two authorities hold the same views, and such evidence as has been gathered is a tenuous basis for convincing conclusions. It seems probable that the common Chinese names follow more or less vaguely generic distinctions in the botanical sense, and that the great variety in colour, texture, marking and grain represents a wide range of different parts of the log» (Houghton, XXI).

In addition to these distinctions come those of the place of growth and the time of felling. For centuries only the finest and oldest trees were utilised. This accounts for the beautiful quality in grain, streaking and colour of the wood of earlier Chinese furniture. After the best trees had disappeared, logs of inferior quality and perhaps different provenience were used. In fact, this change in the quality of raw material seems to correspond to a decay in the craftsman's inspiration. Here, then, is a vague but still suggestive aid in dating plain Chinese furniture. The modern dealers cannot sufficiently stress the obvious qualities of the old material. The modifier *lao* (old) before the traditional name of the wood, confirmed by other marks of excellence, is one of their principal arguments to impress the customer.

It seems, however, to be certain that the four groups of hardwood that were, and partly still are, employed by the Chinese joiner are *Leguminosae*. All of them have varieties and trade equivalents indigenous to China. Yet, as Hommel has justly stated, the bulk of the timber used for cabinet-work was imported from Indo-China and the Malay regions, probably since the beginning of a Southern oversea colonisation.

The more important of these woods are the various *Pterocarpus* species included in the West under the collective name Rosewood. But the «question of the identity of rosewood has not yet been fully investigated in China. Indeed, rosewood is a term as generally applied as 'ironwood' and to almost as great a variety of plants in different parts of the world. Most of the rosewoods, of which there are more than thirty kinds, have heavy, dark coloured woods, and many belong to the *Leguminosae*, in such genera as *Dalbergia* and *Pterocarpus*» (XXI, Houghton, after Norman Shaw).

Tzu-t'an 紫檀

Tzut'an is unanimously considered by the Chinese to be the most distinguished cabinet wood. Among the objects of the Shosoin are shown articles made of this wood, which were imported from China before the middle of the eighth century (Fig. 11). Yet the history of the use of hard t'an wood in China certainly goes back much further, as the references, collected by Bretschneider and referable only to an indigenous Chinese wood, prove beyond question (III).

Most experts now agree in identifying tzut'an as *Pterocarpus santalinus* (red sandalwood, red sanders, palisander). A publication of the Chinese Maritime Customs (XL, p. 524) states that the «wood is exceedingly hard and has a coarse, dense grain and a bright surface. It is of a reddish brown to red colour, due to the presence of 'santalin', a colouring matter...» Naturally, this cabinet wood has nothing in common with the fragrant white sandalwood (*Santalinum* species) except the character *t'an* in Chinese and the misleading Western designation. *Pterocarpus santalinus* is not indigenous to China, but is found in the tropical forests of India and the Sunda Islands.

Duhalde, on the other hand, classifies tzut'an as a *Dalbergia* species and says that «no kind of wood, for beauty, can equal the tzut'an; it is a reddish black and full of fine veins, which seem almost painted. It is very proper for cabinets and the finest sort of joiner's work, and whatever is made of it is held in great esteem.» Dr. Houghton, to whom I am indebted for this passage, remarks that «the source of tzut'an is obscure. If it is *Dalbergia*, it is probably *D. benthamii*, since the other members of the Genus found in China are small trees or shrubs, with the exception of *D. hupeana*, the wood of which is yellow in colour and is used only for the making of wheel hubs and the like. The problem of whether tzut'an as used through the centuries is *Pterocarpus* or *Dalbergia* must continue to be a controversial one until the experts can arrive at some accord.

The two genera are closely allied in any case, so that the question becomes in part a historical one» (XXI).

For the time being we may assume that both *Pterocarpus santalinus* and *Dalbergia benthamii* have been traded in China under the same name, tzut'an; that in earlier times the indigenous *Dalbergia* species was used; and that it was gradually, but never entirely, replaced by the imported *Pterocarpus santalinus*. The English Note to Volume VII of the Catalogue of the Imperial Treasures in the Shosoin (LIII) says about the box with stand illustrated there on Plates 19 to 21, that it is made of «black persimmon-wood, stained with sapan juice» — perhaps to imitate tzut'an. A sample of Ming tzut'an is shown in photograph 3ᵃ on Pl. 18. What I have seen of red sandalwood furniture discloses a very heavy, close-grained, and highly elastic wood wich is extremely hard; it has almost no figure. Through waxing, polishing, and the oxidation of centuries, it has taken on a brownish violet or blackish violet colour; its intact surface displays a rich satin-like lustre (Pl. 2).

Hua-li 花 梨

From the days of the Sung Dynasty, or even earlier, until the beginning of the Ch'ing Dynasty high-grade Huali Wood used to be the common raw material for domestic cabinet-work. As several varieties go under the same trade name, this wood offers still more 'complicated problems of botanical identification. It comprises the exquisite *huang-hua-li* 黃花梨 of Ming and of Early Ch'ing pieces; the dull *lao-hua-li* 老花梨, with its brownish yellow hues, used much in later plain furniture especially during the first part of the nineteenth centur; and the *hsin-hua-li* 新花梨, really of the hungmu group. The last-named is now used in copying early furniture. Indigenous and imported varieties of huali seem to have been used since the Ming period without any clear distinction. The Chinese wood traded under this name has been identified as *Ormosia henryi*, native to Chekiang, Kiangsi, Hupeh, Yünnan, and Kwangtung. Dr. Y. Tang calls it «one of the most important timber trees in China» and describes its wood as «heartwood, dark reddish-brown, sapwood... pinkish-brown; close-grained, fine in texture, very hard and very heavy; with few radial fissures when air-dried» (XXXVI). In Chao Ju-kua's treatise on the Chinese and Arab Trade in the Twelfth and Thirteenth Centuries (IV), a kind of imported wood is mentioned that obviously belongs to the huali group in a later, wider sense of the trade name. «Musk-wood comes from Annam and Cambodia..., as its fragrance has a slight resemblance to that of musk, the wood is called 'musk-wood'...

The people of Chüanchow (Fukien) use this wood a good deal for making of furniture resembling that made of (huali) rosewod.» Thus, a thirteenth century expert still makes a distinction between the indigenous real huali and an aromatic wood that only resembles the genuine Chinese variety, but was imported from the South. Cases and cabinets of Ming or Early Ch'ing character, our pieces 103 and 105 for instance, prescrve to this day a strong sweet fragrance, which proves their wood to be of the rosewood group. Whether, or not, *Ormosia henryi* and other Chinese *Leguminosae* lack this finer aromatic quality, I have not been able to find out. It might be one of the ways to arrive at a more exact determination of the indigenous and of imported varieties.

Interesting is a subsequent remark by the Sung author that the same tree, when it falls from age and decays in the ground, provides the best quality of 'musk-wood'. This leads us to believe that the log was purposely left in the ground to undergo a maturing and discolouring process through humification, which might account for the pleasant odour and the rich dark tints of much of the older huali furniture.

Samples taken from early huali pieces were identified as sub-species of *Pterocarpus indicus;* none, so far, as *Ormosia henryi*. Therefore one may be justified in assuming that most of the huali was imported, the Chinese equivalent being used perhaps only for local cabinet-making, but that it later provided the trade name for this wole group of rosewoods.

The wood of old huali furniture is generally specified as 'yellow' (huang), to describe the tinge of colour common to all genuine pieces, whether light or oxidised. A golden shimmer appears in this tone, as though reflected from a foil, and suffuses the polished surface with a strange glow of beauty.

The horse-hoof foot of Plate 1 indicates what may have been the Ming ideal of the best huali. It is amber-coloured, densely grained, and tends to have eyes and knots; it has a darker streaking, and an expressive, sometimes grotesque, linear figure. Now and then one may observe in the wood a mottled and clouded quality which would indicate an Amboyna variety.

Hung-mu 紅木

Old Hungmu, as known from Ch'ienlung pieces, is likewise identified as a sub-species of *Pterocarpus indicus*. Its black-red quality, enhanced through the wax polish and through maturing, may have brought it into fashion as a substitute for the costly red sandalwood. Its use has become general only since the early eighteenth century, as far as one is able to judge from datable pictures which support the evidence of extant furniture (cf. pieces 5, 73, 88 of our collection). A careful comparison of the rich material offered in the two works quoted under (XLVI) and (XLVII) would be interesting; the former from which our frontispiece is taken, is of typical Ming character, while the latter shows an eighteenth century adaptation of the same furniture. Most of the later forms lie outside the scope of this book, as they develop a style which is essentially different from that of the preceding huang-huali period.

We include here a discussion of hungmu, since modern cabinet-makers employ the lighter coloured varieties, as said above, in imitating old huali furniture. Through proper treatment the so-called hsin-huali of the hungmu group can be made to appear somewhat like a real huali variety darkened through age. But neither the golden foil, nor the markings of genuine huang-huali wood, can be artificially produced, as may be seen by comparing photographs 97*a* and 109*a* (Pl. 160); the former shows a hungmu, the latter a huang-huali specimen.

The Customs publication (XL, p. 509) identifies hungmu with still another wood, that of *Adenanthera pavonina* «which grows in the moist forests of Bengal, Assam, Bombay and Burma. The wood, which is sometimes called 'red sandalwood' or 'coral wood', is dark red in colour, fine-grained and heavy.» Perhaps also one of the various kinds of 'blackwood' may go in the market under the name hungmu, namely the so-called Indian Rosewood, *Dalbergia latifolia*, about which the Customs publication remarks that «produced chiefly in India, it is a reddish or purple-brown wood streaked with black; it has a fragrant, rose-like odour... and an even but fairly coarse and open grain. It is used chiefly in making high-grade furniture» (XL, p. 512).

The sub-species of *Pterocarpus indicus* from which the common kind of hungmu still is obtained, grows in Southern China and South Eastern Asia. In the West it used to go, and is partly still known, under the name Padauk, which seems to include huali varieties (XXXV). In a narrower sense it is now commonly called 'Andaman Redwood'; 'Burmese Rosewood'; and 'Narra' in the Philippine Islands. The Customs publication says of it that the «heart-wood, which constitutes the timber of commerce, is reddish-brown, dark red to rich red, or crimson in colour, and sometimes streaked with black... It is smooth, close-grained, cold to the touch, fairly hard and very durable, possessing a slight aromatic scent... It is very easily worked, takes a fine polish and is used chiefly for the making of furniture.» (XL, p. 483). Dr. Houghton remarks on hungmu that it «is a generic term applied to rosewoods somewhat coarser in texture and lighter in weight than tzut'an. The colour varies not only with the particular strain of the wood, but also with age. Generally these types are used as substitutes, in whole or part, for the choicer kinds of rosewood. However, many of them are beautiful in marking, and durable. Their chief defect is a tendency to accomodate readily to changes in temperature and moisture by shrinkage or swelling» (XXI).

Chi-ch'ih-mu 鷄翅木 (Ch'i-tʒu-mu 杞梓木)

Chich'ihmu is by far the most masculine of all hardwoods utilised by the Chinese cabinet-maker. In intrinsic strength it is superior to the oak of Gothic and Renaissance furniture. Its higher grades possess a peculiar, almost uncouth, figure and a lighter, very marked grain (Pl. 54). Its variegated tones of grayish brown darken with age and may turn through the exposure of centuries into a deep coffee-colour. The craftsman understood the austere nature of this wood and, for its sake, modified the standard types and ornaments (Pls. 26, 55, 69).

The popular name «Chicken-wing Wood» seems to refer to the characteristic gray-brown and the dark streaks of the wood, much as the name «Partridge Wood» for *Andira inermis,* is descriptive of appearance. But again, the botanical attribution proves to be difficult. Once more different woods seem to come under the same trade name. A sample, similar to that on Pl. 54, was identified by Dr. H. Hattori as *Cassia siamea Lam. (Leguminosae);* while the slightly different wood employed for pieces later in form, still now available in the market, is identified by Chinese experts as *Ormosia hosiei,* the *hung-tou* 紅豆 tree of Central and Western China (XXI). Professor Woon Young Chun describes its wood as «reddish, handsomely marked, hard and heavy, one of the most valuable woods for furniture and carving» (XLI). A slight pinkish tone and a weaker veinage seem to distinguish this indigenous Chinese species from the imported *Caesalpiniacea* species of earlier chich'ihmu furniture.

METAL MOUNTS

Metal mounts are to Chinese furniture what ormolus are to the Rococo. Wardrobes, cabinets, and chests of drawers derive much of their beauty from the distribution of such fittings, which sometimes seems to have been accomplished with a knowledge of the Medial Section.

Colour and finish distinguish the genuine mounts from those made of imported brass with their machine-made polish. Two typical old metal fragments were analysed in the Chemical Department of the Catholic University, Peking. One had a silvery; the other, a light yellow colour. Both samples represent a sort of paktong (*pai-t'ung* 白銅), a copper-nickel-zinc alloy, which corresponds to the German-silver of Western metallurgy, the difference being due to the varying amounts of its constituents. That these alloys were not produced from a suitably proportioned mixture of the pure constituents seems certain. In the course of an age-long practice, the Chinese metal-workers must have found out empirically certain ore mixtures which in smelting yield these peculiar alloys. It is probable even that there exist in China localities where the ores of the three constituents occur associated together. In the determination of the alloys of early bronzes, similar possibilities have been weighed. In our case we must remember that « nickeliferous alloys were known to the Chinese since ancient times, while in Europe pure nickel was isolated only as late as 1751 » (XIX). German-silver, in general, is characterised by a relatively high melting point and good malleability. In China, as Hommel has pointed out (XX, p. 20), metals as copper and paktong are cast in sheets and then worked in the cold state. An inherited experience and a natural skill enabled the Chinese craftsman to produce that density of texture which is typical of hammered paktong and a main prerequisite of its mellow, slowly tarnishing lustre. The latter combines with the delicate colour tones, making these mounts the appropriate complements of plain old rosewood furniture.

The forms of the fittings speak to the eyes and require no interpretation (Pls. 156-160). It is noteworthy, however, that none of the geometrical types were adopted by the Western ebonists of the eighteenth century. Only the bat (97[a]) found its way to Rococo Europe and to Colonial America. There its bizarre pattern was turned upside down and still further distorted, to serve as a model for one of the most common escutcheon designs.

The lock and handle plates are held in place by flattened wires thrust through small drilled holes and clinched into the wood of the interior surface. On the outer surface of drawers, or frame pieces, these wires serve as loops for handles and pulls, or they are part of the massive loop pieces for the padlocks (Pl. 124, cross-section; Pl. 133, right top). The hinge plates are fastened with separate cotter pins, ground flush, or provided with ornamental heads (105, 100, Pl. 156). The wires are very strong, being made of the same tough paktong material.

CRAFTSMANSHIP — ORNAMENT — DATING.

A Berlin inventory of the eighteenth century says of an ornate Chinese huang-huali tester bed (XXXI) in the former Electoral Collection: «The curiosity of the bedstead consists in the fact that no nail has been employed in its construction. Also in every other respect it displays the art and the skill of its maker. Its wood is supposed to emanate a delicate scent which, however, has almost vanished in the course of time» (XXXII). It is the quality of wood and craftsmanship that impressed the Western expert of an age that still preserved a sound tradition. He saw at once the pure wood-work, which is so distinctive a feature of traditional Chinese joinery. We too have so far endeavoured to draw attention to the excellence of earlier Chinese cabinet-work, to its costly simplicity and the perfection of its finish. May we now add, or repeat, a few points worth remembering.

No wooden pins, unless absolutely necessary; no glue, where it may be avoided; no turning wheresoever — these are three fundamental rules of the Chinese cabinet-maker.

Among our examples there is only Piece 14 in which, to secure the four principal joints, dowel pins were found to be indispensable (Pl. 16; Pl. 152, Joint 4). With their cross-grain ends, they have been left visible as dark, circular spots on the lighter surface. In some cases the wooden nails seem to be later additions to help fasten the joints after dissecting and re-assembling. The grappling of the oblique braces to the clamp requires the help of strong dowels (Joint 18ᵃ, Pl. 154). Metal nails are, naturally, out of the question. The use of glue was permitted only in rare instances, as when adding feet underneath a bottom frame (pieces 6, 71, 110, 112), when strengthening housed dovetails (Joint 15, Pl. 153), or fixing an ornamental frame to a sunken panel (Pl. 120). The turning lathe was, and still is, despised as unworthy of a skilled worker. Most of the rounded members are more or less ovoid in section (Pl. 47). Even today such bars and uprights are worked by eye and hand out of the log, the tool being a simple drawing knife similar to the old-fashioned Western spoke-shave (XX, Fig. 363).

Cabriole legs (pieces 3, 3ᵃ, 20, 110), club-feet (pieces 6, 15) and oblique braces (pieces 6, 7) are true scuplture, carved without parsimony out of the solid material. The elasticity of the rosewoods made possible, on the other hand, not only intricate and daring joints, but also that steel-like slenderness or muscular vigour which are the outstanding features of Chinese structural design.

In his respect for organic substance the Chinese woodworker never veneered, except in the cheaper furniture not meant to last. The bamboo veneer of Piece 68 (Pl. 89) is quite an extraordinary example only bound to reveal this very feeling for the nature of the wood.

For the finish of the higher grades of hardwood furniture no colouring matter was added to the wax-polish. Occasionally a thin transparent lacquer seems to have been used. The maturing of colour and lustre was left to time, unless the timber had been previously treated. After centuries of handling, an old surface of rosewood may present an appearance impossible to obtain in any other way. The metallic gloss, the absence of sharp edges, and a modulated relief endow some ancient Chinese pieces with a character rarely met with in the furniture of any other style (Pl. 60).

The early embellishments agree with the intrinsic character of the mode of construction. Bends, beads and mouldings, delicate or bold carvings, are not external additions but an organic part of the total design (pieces 37, 55, 60 a. o.). One might say that the difference between the plain early pieces and those of a later decorated style would correspond to that between the reticence of early porcelain and the splendour of certain Ch'ing polychrome productions. In fact, a new order of taste must have made its appearance with examples like the bed in the Berlin Collection (XXXI), which is covered with carving. It seems as typically K'anghsi, as bed 23 may be of the early seventeenth century, and the huge alcove bed 26, of the fifteenth; (cf. the late and ornate examples in I, p. 149; VI, Pls. 38-41; XXIV, Fig. 62).

Throughout our discussion of representative examples attempts have been made to give some idea as to the period of their make, although about their exact date we know next to nothing. To arrange our material in a correct chronological order seems to be impossible. And yet, the experienced Chinese dealer is ready enough to speak of 'Early Ming', 'Late Ming', 'Seventeenth Century', 'Late K'anghsi', and 'Ch'ienlung'. What marks enable him to make these attributions? Some arguments we have already utilised. Without going into details, these and our own observations may now be summed up. They are vague enough, but still offer indices of age, often of pre-seventeenth century workmanship:

The size of the wood, not available at later periods; the richness of figure and grain; a matured colour; the time-wrought lustre of an intact surface; the quality of the metal mounts.

Some typical technical features, such as the protective lining of the interior surface with light-coloured lacquer; an external black lacquer coating with characteristic longitudinal fissures (Pls. 8, 58, 62, 116); the use of coloured Yünnan («Tali») marble slabs as panels of the table top (Pl. 70; cf. XL, p. 456).

An unerring sense of proportion; a rigid or subtle, but always functional conception of form, inseparable from the meaning of the structure.

Certain elements of ornamentation seem to permit still further conclusions. Trestle table 66 (Pl. 87) is here particularly valuable, since it has a given date. Produced at the very end of the Ming Dynasty, it helps to understand the style of the seventeenth century. From the forms of its apron one may go forward and backward; scrolls similarly softened and simplified occur in a related side table whose huali wood seems to indicate an even later, probably a K'anghsi date (Piece 67, Pl. 88). How much strength the traditional scrolls of these two tables have lost is seen in the brackets of pieces 65, 64 and 63, taken in the order given. Considering the apparent evolution of this motif, as well as features of patina and general design, one may date table 65 (Pl. 86) as early as the sixteenth century and bench 64 (Pl. 83) around fifteen hundred.

Table 63, however, reveals perfection. It is unique in the mature honey colour of the wood and the gloss of the surface; in its composition; in the powerful modelling of the openwork; in the vigorously pointed ogee arches; in the relief of the edge beads; in the calligraphic precision of the scrolled and pointed brackets (Pl. 82).

The table might be a work of the fifteenth century. The form of its scrolls (cf. Pl. 45) occurs somewhat weaker in the offering table of a sixteenth century ancestral hall at Chüanchow (Pl. 161), and is still further reduced in lacquer tables of the seventeenth and eighteenth centuries (XXXIII, Pls. 33-35). As late as the Ch'ienlung period this side table with scrolled brackets has not yet died out. Evolved through three centuries, the design is now carried out with the frigid but cultured taste of an almost worn-out tradition (Piece 68, Pl. 89).

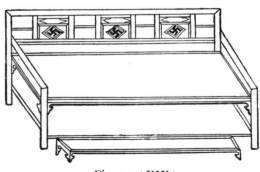

Fig. 24 (XIX)

We here return for a last word about the surviving traces of the ancient panel openings (Figs. 5, 6). Fig. 24 is drawn from a wood-cut of the Yüan Dynasty. This couch with railing, in the style of the time, is important for several reasons. Of a typically transitional character, it proves to be a predecessor of Ming couch 16 (Pl. 20). The latter excells through the harmony of its unified design. The composition of the lattice-work in the Yüan piece, however, seems to be still in the experimental stage, and the railing does not yet definitely fuse into a homogeneous whole with the platform. The companion foot-stool has open scroll feet in the Sung style, and not the solid horse-hoof of Early Ming. The scrolled apron brackets of the Yüan couch are likewise remnants of the ancient panel cutouts. While such brackets with beading are not found in couch 16, they appear in table 10 and cabinet 92, and, in simplified form, in the back-rests of chair 84 (Pls. 11, 113, 105). They connect these three pieces with the Yüan style. A vigorous design and the superior quality of material; the matured hue of the finished wood; the oblique braces of the table and its fully developed horse-hoofs may thus justify an attribution of pieces 10, 84, and 92 to Early Ming. The legs and feet of table 10 with their exquisite contours represent the beginning; the feet of couch 19 (Pl. 25), the end of a final evolution.

CABINET MAKING AFTER YÜAN — RISE AND DECLINE

The spiritual conditions in China under the Yüan Dynasty gave to painting its last and decisive impetus, while architecture and cabinet-making entered into a transformation which was completed later. Indeed, the national impulses of a Chinese dynasty were necessary to bring about a conclusive development of these social arts. Architecture, for the first time since the eighth century, reached a new climax in the beginning of the Ming Dynasty, whereas furniture attained only then its perfection.

The best period of Chinese furniture may coincide with the flourishing time of blue-and-white porcelain, while soon after fifteen hundred the gradual decline seems to have begun. During the later seventeenth century the surviving traditions of the classical Ming style were lost feature after feature. A regulated but often charming delicacy (Piece 114, Pl. 142) now replaces the boldness of the earlier designs. In other cases, as on the Berlin bed, sumptuous carvings encroach upon the natural beauty of the wood and start interfering with the greatness of linear composition.

Then comes the introduction of hungmu, due also, as we assume, to the exhaustion of the supply of nobler rosewoods. The almost exclusive use of huang-huali varieties, associated with the Soochow and Yangchow workshops for centuries, now ceased. This wood had been the peculiar feature of high-grade household furniture during the Ming and, most likely, the two preceding dynasties. When later, towards the end of the eighteenth century, a new demand for lighter coloured woods arose, it was satisfied with the coarse lao-huali that, occasionally, encouraged a weak revival of the plain old taste (pieces 22, 28, 29).

The hungmu style, still refined in the earlier Peking specimens (Piece 5), began to decline definitely with the later part of the Ch'ienlung period. It becomes, lifeless (Piece 73), or gaudy, and finally dies out with the blackwood show pieces of Canton or Shanghai design (XXIV, Figs. 76-82). It is the rustic furniture in native soft woods that has preserved the simple structural form, and a notion of the traditional Chinese sense of proportion.

CONCLUSION

We have an excellent introduction to what was Chinese life under the Later Ch'ing Dynasty in Lin Yutang's admirable rendering of Shen Fu's *Fu-sheng liu-chi* or Six Chapters of a Floating Life (XXXIV). Here we see Chinese domestic culture before the destructive changes wrought in the last century. Even a hundred years ago, Ming tradition lingered on in Soochow families, though today only few houses may be left in all China to give us an idea of the surroundings from which our examples come.

May we suggest a comparison with the Quattro Cento home, as seen in certain paintings, particularly of the Venetian School, for instance in Cima's *Annunciation*, (Hermitage), or in Carpaccio's *Dream of St. Ursula* (Academy). It may help to recapture the recondite charm of a Ming interior. Of this at least the scattered elements remain, and some of them are found in the present collection.

A Ming home of the leisured class, so much we know, displayed an inspired richness in the garb of grave and measured simplicity. The spacious Central Hall was carried on two rows of tall pillars; left and right, east and west, were latticed partitions in cabinet-wood (cf. Pl. 37), dressed at the back with mellow-coloured silks. The walls and pillars were papered. The floor was laid with black polished flagstones, and the ceiling finished with cloisons in yellow reed-work. Against this sombre background the furniture was disposed, subservient to the discipline of the plan. The amber or purple hues of the rosewood pieces agreed with the subdued tones of the costly rugs, of the chair covers and cushions in tapestry or embroidered silk. Pendant scrolls of calligraphies and paintings, blue-and-white porcelains or waxed-green bronzes on red lacquer stands were distributed with studied care. Papered lattice windows kept out the glare of the day, open candles and horn lanterns blended by night the colours in subtle harmony.

Thus, straightforward and luxurious, was the character of a Ming interior. In Fig. 2 we have shown a hall in the taste of the nineteenth century. Then, as throughout the history of domestic life, we find the layout and its furniture ruled by rigid standards. While the Chinese had early developed to perfection the art of cultured ease, the setting of their daily life retains an appearance of archaic austerity (cf. II, LVII). This is what we see in the Frontispiece, a bed chamber in the style of the sixteenth century (XLVI). In this place of rest the furniture is more freely arranged, but it reveals again that restraint in design and ornament, that power of line and cubic proportion which is second nature to the classic Chinese builder. Even in the innermost apartment comfort seems to cede to the sway of Wood, Structure, Dignity.

Fig. 25 (XI)

BIBLIOGRAPHY

Boerschmann, Ernst

    I *Die Baukunst und Religiöse Kultur der Chinesen,* Volume I, Berlin, 1911.

    II *Baukunst und Landschaft in China,* Berlin, 1923, (Pl. 263).

Bretschneider, Emil V.

    III *Botanicon Sinicum, Notes on Chinese Botany from Native and Western Sources,* Part II, Shanghai, 1892, (p. 375).

Chau Ju-kua (Chao Ju-kua 趙汝适)

    IV *Chu-fan-chi* (*Chu-fan-chih* 諸蕃志), translated by F. Hirth & W. W. Rockhill, St. Petersburg, 1911, (p. 212).

Coedès, Georges

    V «L'art de la laque dorée au Siam», in *Revue des Arts Asiatiques,* Tome II, No. 3, 1925, p. 3 sqq., (Pl. 2).

Dupont, Maurice

    VI *Les meubles de la Chine,* Second Series, Paris, 1926.

Dye, Daniel Sheets

    VII *A Grammar of Chinese Lattice,* 2 vols., Cambridge, Mass., 1937.

Ecke, Gustav

    VIII «Sechs Schaubilder Pekinger Innenräume des Achtzehnten Jahrhunderts», in *Bulletin No. 9 of the Catholic University of Peking,* Nov. 1934, p. 155 sqq.

    IX «Wandlungen des Faltstuhls, Bemerkungen zur Geschichte der Eurasischen Stuhlform», in *Monumenta Serica,* Vol. IX, 1944, p. 34 sqq. (Our Fig. 20 is taken from Fig. 10; cf. note 25).

    X *Frühe Chinesische Bronzen aus der Sammlung Oskar Trautmann,* Peking, 1939. (Our Fig. 22 is taken from Pl. 1).

Erdberg Consten, Eleanor von

XI «A Statue of Lao-tzu in the Po-yün-kuan», in *Monumenta Serica,* Vol.VII, 1942, p.235 sqq. (Our Fig.25 is taken from the illustration on p. 240, a Yüan panel ornament traced from the original stone carving by E. v. E. Consten).

Ferguson, John C.

XII «Chinese Furniture», in *Survey of Chinese Art,* Shanghai, 1939, p. 109 sqq., (Fig. 177).

Feulner, Adolf

XIII *Kunstgeschichte des Möbels,* dritte Auflage, Berlin, 1927. (Our Fig.21 is drawn from Fig.207).

Fischer, Otto

XIV *Die Chinesische Malerei der Han-Dynastie,* Berlin, 1931. (Pl.32/33, stone engraving, probably of the first century A. D., from the Sacrificial Hall of Chu Wei 朱鮪, at Chin-hsiang hsien 金祥縣, Shantung; note the mitred frame construction).

Fu Yün-tzu 傅芸子

XV *Cheng-ts'ang-yüan (Shosoin) k'ao-ku-chi* 正倉院考古記 Tokyo, 1941. (Our Fig.10 is reproduced after Fig.24 on p.92).

Grousset, René

XVI *Les civilisations de l'Orient, Tome III, La Chine,* Paris, 1930. (Our motto is taken from p.2).

Hamada Kosaku 濱田耕作

XVII *Senoku seisho* 泉屋清賞 *(The Collection of Old Bronzes of Baron Sumitomo),* Additional Volume (續編), Part I, Kyoto, 1926. (Our Fig.16 is drawn from Pl.192).

Harada Bizan 原田尾山

XVIII *Shina meiga hokan* 支那名畫寶鑒 *(The Pageant of Chinese Painting),* Tokyo, 1936, (Pl. 11).

Hofmann, K. A.

XIX *Lehrbuch der Anorganischen Chemie,* Braunschweig, 1920, (p.623).

Hommel, Rudolf P.

    XX   *China at Work*, New York, 1937.

Houghton, Henry S.

    XXI   *Cabinet Woods (The Principal Types... used in North China for Fine Joinery)*, MS., Peking, 1941.

Huang Chün 黃濬

    XXII   *Yeh-chung p'ien-yü* 鄴中片羽, Third Series (第三集), Peking, 1942. (Our Fig.12 is taken from the first chüan, fol. 16 verso).

Jung Keng 容庚

    XXIII   *Shang Chou i-ch'i t'ung-k'ao* 商周彝器通考 *(The Bronzes of Shang and Chou)*, 2 vols., Peiping, 1941, (Vol. II, p. 98).

Kelling, Rudolf

    XXIV   *Das Chinesische Wohnhaus,* Tokyo, 1935.

Liang Ssu-ch'eng 梁思成 & Liu Chih-p'ing 劉致平

    XXV   *Tien-mien* 店面 (建築設計參考圖集第三集), Society for Research in Chinese Architecture 中國營造學社, Peiping, 1935.

    XXVI   *Tsao-ching* 藻井 (建築設計參考圖集第十集), Peiping, 1937, (Pls.9 and 24, left).

Lin-ch'ing 麟慶

    XXVII   *Hung-hsüeh yin-yüan t'u-chi* 鴻雪因緣圖記, edition of 1847, three series in six volumes. (Our Fig. 2 is reproduced after «Nan-yang fang-chiu» 南陽訪舊 in the first volume of the second series).

Maspero, Henri

    XXVIII   «La vie privée en Chine à l'époque des Han», in *Revue des Arts Asiatiques,* Tome VII, No.4, 1932, p.185 sqq.

Omura Seigai 大村西崖

    XXIX   *Bunjinga sen* 文人畫選, Second Series, First Volume (第二輯第一冊), Tokyo, 1922. (Our Fig.17 is drawn from Pl.1, «Fu-sheng Lecturing on the Book of History» 伏生授經圖卷, painted by Wang Wei 王維).

Reichwein, Adolf

    XXX   *China und Japan im Achtzehnten Jahrhundert,* Berlin, 1923, (Pl.12).

Reidemeister, Leopold

    XXXI «Der Grosse Kurfürst und Friedrich III. als Sammler Ostasia-tischer Kunst», in *Ostasiatische Zeitschrift,* Neue Folge Achter Jahrgang, 1932, p.175 sqq., (Pl.23).

    XXXII *China und Japan in der Kunstkammer der Brandenburgischen Kurfürsten,* Ausstellungskatalog, Berlin, 1932, (p.21).

Roche, Odilon

    XXXIII *Les meubles de la Chine,* First Series, Paris, 1925.

Shen Fu 沈復

    XXXIV *Fu-sheng liu-chi* 浮生六記, translated by Lin Yutang 林語堂 in the *T'ien Hsia Monthly,* Vol.I, Nos. 1-4, Aug.-Nov., 1935; reprinted with the Chinese text by Hsi-feng-shê 西風社 Shanghai, 1941.

Slomann, Wilhelm

    XXXV «Chinesische Möbel des Achtzehnten Jahrhunderts», in *Pantheon,* Jahrgang 1929, drittes Heft, März, p.142 sqq.

Tang, Y. (T'ang Yüeh 唐燿)

    XXXVI «Identifications of Some Important Hardwoods of South China by their Gross Structure», in *Bulletin of the Fan Memorial Institute of Biology,* Vol.III, No.17, Peiping, Nov. 1932, (p.300).

Tomita Kojiro

    XXXVII Museum of Fine Arts, Boston, *Portfolio of Chinese Paintings in the Museum (Han to Sung Periods),* Descriptive Text by Kojiro Tomita, Cambridge, Mass., 1933, (Pl.48).

Tchang Yi-tchou & J. Hackin

    XXXVIII *La peinture chinoise au Musée Guimet,* Paris, 1910. (Our Fig.5 is drawn from Pl.1, top).

Umehara Sueji 梅原末治

    XXXIX *Shina kodo seikwa* 支那古銅精華, Part I, Bronze Vessels, Vol. I, Osaka, 1933. (Our Fig.3 is adapted from Pl.9).

Watson, Ernest

XL   *The Principal Articles of Chinese Commerce,* The Maritime
       Customs, II, Special Series: No.38, Second Edition,
       Shanghai, 1930.

Woon Young Chun

XLI   *Chinese Economic Trees,* Shanghai, 1921, (p.187).

Wu Jung 午榮 & Chang Yen 章嚴

XLII   *Lu Pan ching* 魯班經; the edition here used seems to be Late
       Ming. (Our Fig. 1 is taken from chüan 2, fol. 22 recto).

Yetts, W. Perceval

XLIII *The George Eumorfopoulos Collection Catalogue of the Chinese
       and Corean Bronzes...,* 3 vols., London, 1929-1932. (Our
       Fig.9 is drawn from Vol. II, Pl. 58).

Anonymous

XLIV   *Bijutsu kenkyu* 美術研究 *(The Journal of Art Studies),* No. XXV,
       Jan. 1934. (Our Fig. 19 is drawn from Pl. 2).

XLV   No. XCI, July 1939. (Our Fig. 4 is adapted from Pl. I, «Portrait
       of Confucius», an anonymous Japanese painting in the T'ang
       style, and from the above-mentioned Boston *Portfolio,*
       (XXXVII), Pl. 48, as well as from a photograph of a T'ang
       bronze stand, dated 723 A. D., in the collection of Mr.
       Huang Chün 黄濬, Peking).

XLVI   *Chin-p'ing-mei tz'u-hua* 金瓶梅詞話, photographic reproduction
       by the Metropolitan Library of Peiping. (Our Frontispiece
       is adapted from Illustration 97 verso).

XLVII *Ch'ing-kung chen-pao pi-mei-t'u* 清宮珍寶阺美圖, five vols., col-
       lotype edition of about 1930.

XLVIII *Catalogue of the International Exhibition of Chinese Art, 1935-36,*
       Fifth Edition, London. (Our Fig.15 is drawn from No. 63).

XLIX   *Ku-kung chou-k'an* 故宮周刊, No.359, June 16th, 1934. (Our
       Fig. 24 is adapted from an illustration to the Yüan edition
       of the *Shih-lin kuang-chi* 事林廣記, reproduced on p. 916).

L   *The Tomb of Painted Basket of Lo-lang* (樂浪彩篋塚). The Society
       of the Study of Korean Antiquities, Keijo (Seoul), 1934.

LI   *Catalogue of Art Treasures of Ten Great Temples of Nara, Volume Seven, The Horyuji Temple, Part* 7 (大都十大寺大鏡第七輯,法隆寺大鏡,第七), Tokyo, 1933. (Our Fig.18 is adapted from Pls.18 and 30).

LII *Shen-chou kuo-kuang-chi* 神州國光集, Fourth Series (第四集), Portrait of Wang Shih-cheng 王士禎 painted by Yü Chih-ting 禹之鼎 (禹慎齋畫漁洋山人禪悅圖小像).

LIII *Catalogue of the Imperial Treasures in the Shosoin* (正倉院御物圖錄), Tokyo, Vol. I, 1929; II, 1932; VII, 1934; IX, 1936. (Our Fig. 23 is drawn from Vol. I, Pl. 17).

LIV *Showa gonendo koseki chosa hokoku* 昭和五年度古蹟調査報告, published in 1935 by the Government-General of Korea.

LV   *Toei juko* 東瀛珠光, Fifth Series (第五輯), Second Edition, Tokyo, 1927. (Our Fig. 11 is drawn from Pl. 281).

LVI *Wan-shou sheng-tien* 萬壽盛典, First Series (初集), chüan 40, (fol. 37, verso).

LVII *Wen-yüan-ko ts'ang-shu ch'üan-ching* 文淵閣藏書全景, published by the Society for Research in Chinese Architecture, Peiping, 1935. (See the plate showing the interior view of the upper story, 文淵閣內部上層御榻).

LVIII «Catalogue of Baron Kuga and Mr. Shimada Collections» (男爵久我家並島田家所藏品入札), auctioned at the Bijutsu Club of Tokyo (東京美術俱樂部) on Sept. 23rd, 1929. (Our Fig.6 is adapted from No.92, and from a similar lacquer stand in the Palace Museum, Peking).

LIX «Catalogue of an Anonymous Collection» (某家所藏品入札) auctioned at the Bijutsu Club of Tokyo on Dec. 4th, without indication of year. (Our Fig. 7 is drawn from No. 416).

NOTE

CHINESE NAMES: The Peking vernacular makes no consistent distinction of form and use. There are six main groups of furniture:

1. Couches and Beds.

Plain couches are called *t'a* 榻; couches with railing, or full beds, *ch'uang* 牀; the expressions *hu-ch'uang* 胡牀, or *lo-han-ch'uang* 羅漢牀, are still in use for the railed couch; the term for a canopy frame, *chia-tzu* 架子, is added to specify a testered bedstead. The term *k'ang* 炕, not common for movable platforms, is used to specify couch tables.

2. Tables.

Names for tables are: *chi* 几, for a small table, low or high, derived from the box construction; *cho* 桌, a collective for various tables, usually large and square; and *an* 案, for long and narrow tables. The modifier *fang* 方 indicates square, *yüan* 圓, round, *t'iao* 條, small and oblong structures; *pa-hsien* 八仙, *liu-hsien,* 六仙, and *ssu-hsien* 四仙, are common modifiers to specify larger or smaller high, square tables. In speaking of table tops, *p'ing-t'ou* 平頭 refers to plain tops; *ch'iao-t'ou* 翹頭 to those with up-turned ends. Large, oblong tables used in the study are called *shu-an* 書案; dressing tables (cf. Frontispiece of Introduction), with front drawers, usually three, are called *san-t'i-cho* 三屜桌; semicircular tables, reminiscent, and perhaps models, of the Western pier-table, are called *yüeh-ya-cho* 月牙桌. Following a suggestion of Mr. John Hope-Johnstone, the translation 'psaltery table' has been adopted for *ch'in-cho* 琴桌. Compound trestle tables with separate supporting stands *(chi)* are called *chia-chi-an* 架几案.

3. Seats.

Among the seats, the bench is called *teng* 凳; the square stool, *wu-teng* 兀凳; the round stool, *tun* 墩; the chair, *i* 椅. For chairs, the modifier *kuan-mao* 官帽 refers to a yoke-back without arm-rests; armchairs are called *fu-shou-i* 扶手椅; chairs with circular rest, *ch'üan-i* 圈椅. The folding chair, *chiao-i* 交椅, has been discussed in a special article (Bibliography, IX). The footstool, *chiao-t'a* 脚踏, may be mentioned here; it is a derivative of the primitive platform construction.

4. Cases and cabinets.

High cases, cupboards and larger cabinets are called *kuei* 櫃; a common specification of splay-leg cabinets, usually with rounded uprights and rails, is *yüan-chiao* 圓脚; *li* 立, *shu* 豎, and *ting-shu* 頂豎, are modifiers for high or compound cabinets and wardrobes; compound cases in four parts are *ssu-chien-kuei* 四件櫃, or simply *ta-kuei* 大櫃. Coffers and smaller cabinets are called *ch'u* 廚; the high-standing splay-leg coffers are known as *men-hu-ch'u* 門戶廚. *Lien-erh-ch'u* 連二廚 and *lien-san-ch'u* 連三廚 represent the cupboard-like evolution of this coffer. A *hsiang* 箱 is a chest with horizontal cover, box-like.

5. Stands.

According to the construction, stands may be called *chi* 几, *t'ai* 臺, or *chia* 架; *p'en-chia* 盆架, and *i-chia* 衣架, are distinguished; candle stands with lanterns are called *chu-t'ai* 燭臺. Racks are always *chia*. The round stools also serve as stands; according to the form imitated they are called *kua-leng-tun* 瓜楞墩, and *ku-erh-tun* 鼓兒墩.

6. Screens.

Of the various well-known kinds of screen, *p'ing* 屏, usually with ornate panels, our collection brings no example.

WOODS: The Reader who is not interested in the botanical names given after the Chinese in the present list, may conveniently use the following equivalents: red sandal-wood for tzut'an; rosewood for the huali and hungmu varieties; and 'chicken-wing' wood for chich'ihmu. A full discussion on the subject is given in the Introduction.

LIST OF PIECES

MEASUREMENTS ARE IN CENTIMETERS

Jt = joints; Ht = height; Pty = property

---

1 Couch table, *k'ang-chi;* tzut'an (*Pterocarpus santalinus*).
Pl 2
Jt 1, 2, 6; Ht 35; top 89 × 67,5.
Pty of Dr. H. S. Houghton

2 Couch table, *k'ang-chi;* huang-huali (*Pterocarpus indicus*).
Measured drawings. Pls 3 top, 4
Jt 1, 2, 6; Ht 29; top 87 × 60.
Pty of Mr. L. C. S. Sickman

3 Couch table, *k'ang-chi;* huang-huali.
Pl 3 bottom
Jt. 1, 2, 6; Ht 28; top 99 × 66.
Pty of Mme Henri Vetch

3ᵃ Foot of square couch table; tzut'an; c. actual size.
Pl 18 right
Pty of the Author

4 Bench, *t'iao-teng;* huang-huali.
Pl 5
Jt 1, 2, 6; Ht 52; top 124 × 52; one of a pair.
Pty of Dr. Ilse Martin

5 Occasional (tea) table, *ch'a-chi;* hungmu (*Pterocarpus indicus*).
Pl 6 left
Jt 1, 2; Ht 85; top 50 × 40.
Pty of Messrs. Robert and William Drummond

6 Occasional (tea) table, *ch'a-chi;* huang-huali.
Measured drawings. Pls 6 right, 7, 18 left
Jt 1, 2, 18, 19, 20; Ht 84; top 55 × 48; suspending cover in drawing restored.
Pty formerly of Prof. Robert Winter, and later of Prof. A. L. Pollard-Urquhart

7 Square table, *fang-cho;* huang-huali. Pl 8
Jt 1, 3, 18, 19; original Ht c. 80, actual Ht 42; top 85 × 85.
Pty of Oberreichsbahnrat H. J. v. Lochow

8 Side table, *t'iao-chi;* huang-huali; detail only; cf. Piece 9.
Pl 9
Jt 1, 3, 19; Ht 81,5; top 81 × 33.
Pty of the Author

9 Side table, *t'iao-an;* huang-huali. Pl 10
Jt 1, 3, 19; Ht 81; top 223,5 × 63.
Pty of Prof. and Mrs. H. F. MacNair

10 Square table, *fang-cho;* huang-huali. Pl 11
Jt 1, 2, 6, 19; Ht 82; top 82 × 82.
Pty of Dr. Mathias Komor

11 Square table, *fang-cho;* huang-huali. Pl 12
Jt 10, 16, 19; Ht 84; top 104 × 104.
Pty of Mme Henri Vetch

12 Square table, *fang-cho;* huang-huali. Pl 13
Jt 1, 2, 6, 16; Ht 82; top 104 × 104.
Pty of John Hope-Johnstone, Esq.

13 Side table, *t'iao-cho;* huang-huali. Pl 14
Jt 1, 2, 6; Ht 87; top 158 × 53.
Pty of Mme Henri Vetch

14 Psaltery table, *ch'in-cho;* huang-huali.
Measured drawings. Pls 15, 16, 17 left
Jt 1, 4; Ht 79; top 144 × 47.
Pty of the Author

14ᵃ Foot of psaltery table in red lacquer.
Pl 17 right
Cf. Odilon Roche, **Les Meubles de la Chine**, Pl XXXVI.
Pty of the Author

15 Couch, *t'a;* huang-huali. Pls 1, 19
Jt 1, 2, 6, 27; Ht 47,5; seat, over all, 197 × 105.
Pty of Herr J. Plaut

16 Couch, *ch'uang;* huang-huali. Pl 20
Jt 1, 2, 6, 16, 27, 28; full Ht 80; Ht of seat 46; seat, over all, 197 × 105.
Pty of Messrs. Robert and William Drummond

17 Couch, *ch'uang;* huang-huali.
Measured drawings. Pls 21-23
Jt 1, 2, 6, 12, 16, 27, 28; actual Ht 77, 5; restored full Ht c. 80; restored Ht of seat c. 46; seat, over all, 204 × 94.
Pty of the Author

18 Couch, *ch'uang;* huang-huali. Pl 24
Jt 1, 2, 6, 12, 16, 27, 28; full Ht 97; Ht of seat 47; seat, over all, 200,5 × 104,5.
Pty of M. Jean Pierre Dubosc

19 Couch, *ch'uang;* huang-huali. Pl 25
Jt 1, 2, 12, 27, 28; full Ht 97; Ht of seat 48; seat, over all, 209 × 126
Pty of Messrs. Robert and William Drummond

20 Couch, *ch'uang;* chich'ihmu (*Cassia siamea*).
Pl 26
Jt 1, 2, 16, 27, 28; full Ht 81; Ht of seat 48; seat, over all, 217 × 120.
Pty of Frl. Editha Leppich

21 Couch, *ch'uang;* huang-huali. Pl 27
Jt 1, 2, 6, 27, 28; full Ht 74; Ht of seat 47; seat, over all, 207 × 94,5.
Pty of Dr. Otto Burchard

22 Couch, *ch'uang;* lao-huali (*Pterocarpus indicus*).
Pl 28
Jt 1, 2, 6, 27, 28; full Ht 108; Ht of seat 55; seat, over all, 199,5 × 125.
Pty of Prof. Walter Fuchs

23 Testered bedstead, *chia-tzu-ch'uang;* huang-huali.
Measured drawings. Pls 29-34
Jt 1, 2, 6, 12, 16, 27; full Ht 242; Ht of seat 52; seat, over all, 226 × 160.
Pty of the Author

24 Testered bedstead, *chia-tzu-ch'uang;* huang-huali.
Pl 35
Jt 1, 2, 6, 27; full Ht 223; Ht of seat 49; seat, over all, 222 × 143.
Pty of Mme Henri Vetch

25 Testered bedstead, *chia-tzu-ch'uang;*
huang-huali.   Pl 36
Jt 1, 2, 12, 27; full Ht 233; Ht of seat 50;
seat, over all, 232 × 168,5.
Pty of Messrs. Robert and William Drummond

26 Alcove bedstead, *ta-ch'uang;* huang-huali.
Pls 37-39
Jt 1, 2, 6, 12, 16, 27; full Ht, with soft-wood dais
and soft-wood tester, 227; full depth 208; Ht
of seat above dais 57; seat, over all, 207 × 141;
frame, without dais and tester, 207 × 207 × 208.
Pty of Sydney M. Cooper, Esq.

27 Footstool, *chiao-t'a;* huang-huali. Pl 40 top
Jt 10; Ht 12,5; top 43,5 × 26,5; one of a pair.
Pty of Prof. Walter Fuchs

28 Footstool, *chiao-t'a;* lao huali. Pl 40 bottom
Jt 10, 24; Ht 11; top 69,5 × 35; one of a pair.
Pty of the Author

29 Ice-box, *ping-hsiang;* lao-huali (?).   Pl 41
Jt 1, 2, 20; full Ht 72; Ht of stand 36; top of
stand, over all, 53 × 53; cover 56 × 56.
Pty of Sydney M. Cooper, Esq.

30 Occasional table, *t'iao-cho;* huang-huali.
Pl 42
Jt 1, 21, 24; Ht 81; top 69 × 39,5.
Pty of Messrs. Robert and William Drummond

31 Bench (low table), *t'iao-teng;* huang-
huali.   Pl 43 bottom
Jt 1, 21, 24; Ht 32; top 82,5 × 57.
Pty of Messrs. Robert and William Drummond

32 Occasional table, *ch'iao-t'ou-an;* huang-
huali.   Pl 44 bottom
Jt 9, 21; single-board top; Ht of board 85,5;
top, over all, 104 × 35.
Pty of Herr J. Plaut

33 Occasional table, *ch'iao-t'ou-an;* huang-
huali.   Pl 44 top
Jt 9, 21, 24; single-board top; Ht of board 85;
top, over all, 99 × 46
Pty of Frau Irene Schierlitz

34 Side table, *ch'iao-t'ou-an;* huang-huali.
Pl 45
Jt 1, 9, 21, 24; Ht of board 84; top, over all,
197 × 49.
Pty of Mme Henri Vetch

35 Occasional table, *t'iao-cho;* huang-huali.
Pl 73 bottom
Jt 1, 23, 24; Ht 82,5; top 119 × 38,5.
Pty of Dr. Mathias Komor

36 Side table, *p'ing-t'ou-an;* huang-huali.
Measured drawings. Pls 46, 47
Jt 1, 7, 23, 24; Ht 82; top 180 × 54.
Pty of Dr. R. J. C. Hoeppli

37 Occasional table, *t'iao-cho;* huang-huali.
Pls 48 top, 49
Jt 1, 23; Ht 75,5; top 86 × 37,5.
Pty of Prof. Walter Fuchs

38 Occasional table with lower shelf, *t'iao-
cho;* huang-huali.   Pl 48 bottom
Jt 1, 21, 24; Ht 79,5; top 88 × 36,5.
Pty of the Author

39 Side table, *p'ing-t'ou-an;* walnut (*Juglans
regia*).   Pl 50
Jt 1, 4; Ht 82,5; top 192 × 59.
Pty of Sydney M. Cooper, Esq.

40 Library table, *shu-an;* huang-huali.
Measured drawings. Pls 51-53
Jt 1, 23; Ht 84; top 165 × 71.
Pty of the Author

41 Library table, *shu-an;* chich'ihmu.
Pls 54, 55
Jt 1, 23, 24; Ht 83; top 272 × 93.
Pty of Mme Henri Vetch

42 Bench (couch), *t'iao-teng;* huang-huali.
Pl 56
Jt 1, 21, 24; Ht 52; seat, over all, 189 × 64.
Pty of Dr. Otto Burchard

43 Side table, *ch'iao-t'ou-an;* huang-huali.
Pl 57
Jt 1, 9, 16, 23; Ht of board 83,5; top, over all,
162 × 35.
Pty of Dr. Otto Burchard

44 Psaltery table, *ch'in-cho;* tzu-t'an   Pl 58
Jt 11; Ht 85; top, over all, 152,5 × 51.
Pty of Dr. John C. Ferguson, who kindly put
at the disposal of the author the photograph
here reproduced; illustrated as Fig. 177 in
John C. Ferguson, **Survey of Chinese Art.**

45 Psaltery table, *ch'in-cho,* huang-huali.
Measured drawings. Pls 59-62
Jt 1, 2; Ht 87; top 145 × 39.
Pty of John Hope-Johnstone, Esq.

46 Bench (low table), *t'iao-teng;* huang-huali.
Pl 43 top
Jt 1, 5, 16; Ht 32; top 89,5 × 30,5.
Pty of H. E. the Italian Ambassador and the
Marchesa Taliani de Marchio

47 Square table, *fang-cho;* huang-huali. Pl 63
Jt 11; Ht 80; top 92 × 92.
Pty of Dr. Otto Burchard

48 Square table, *fang-cho;* huang-huali. Pl 64
Jt 1, 2, 24; Ht 87; top 98 × 98; one of a pair.
Pty of C. M. Skepper, Esq.

49 Occasional table, *t'iao-chi;* huang-huali.
Pl 65 top
Jt 11; Ht 82; top 96 × 53.
Pty of Mme Henri Vetch

50 Occasional table, *t'iao-chi;* huang-huali.
Pl 65 bottom
Jt 1, 2, 16; Ht 87; top 98 × 48,5.
Pty of Dr. Adam v. Trott zu Solz

51 Side table, *t'iao-an;* huang-huali.
Measured drawings. Pls 66-68
Jt 1, 2, 16; Ht 86; top 166 × 62.
Pty of Dr. Adam v. Trott zu Solz

52 Library table, *shu-an;* chich'ihmu.   Pl 69
Jt 11; Ht 85,5; top 177 × 80.
Pty of M. Walter Bosshard

53 Library table *shu-an;* huang-huali with
marble panel; detail only.   Pl 70
Jt 11; Ht 86,5; top 107 × 67,5.
Pty of the Author

54 Square table, *fang-cho;* huang-huali. Pl 71
Jt 11; Ht 80; top 92 × 92.
Pty of Messrs. Robert and William Drummond

55 Side table, semicircular, *yüeh-ya-cho;*
huang-huali. Pl 72 top
Jt 1, 4; Ht 78, 5; diameter of top 84.
Pty of Messrs. Robert and William Drummond

56 Dressing table, *san-t'i-cho;* huang-huali.
Pl 72 bottom
Jt 8, 11; Ht 84; top 102 × 53.
Pty of Messrs. Robert and William Drummond

57 Occasional table, *t'iao-chi;* huang-huali.
Pl 73 top
Jt 1, 2; Ht 83; top 97 × 43, 5.
Pty of Mme Henri Vetch

58 Bench (low table), *t'iao-teng;* huang-huali.
Pl 74 top
Jt 1, 2, 6, 9; Ht 31; top, over all, 81 × 39.
Pty of Dr. Otto Burchard

59 Couch table, *k'ang-chi;* huang-huali.
Pl 74 bottom
Jt 10, 14, 16; Ht 35; top 92 × 36.
Pty of Dr. Otto Burchard

60 Psaltery table, *ch'in-cho;* huang-huali.
Measured drawings. Pls 75-78
Jt 1, 14, 15; single-board top; Ht 79, 5; top
123 × 39, 5.
Pty of Messrs. Robert and William Drummond

61 Side table, *ch'iao-t'ou-an;* huang-huali.
Pls 79, 80
Jt 1, 9, 23; Ht of board 92; top, over all,
243 × 40.
Pty of Prof. Walter Fuchs

61ᵃ Detail of Han Dynasty inkstand in red and
black lacquer. Pl 79 left top
Copy by Mr. Matsui Tamijirō 松井民治郎,
Heijō; cf. **The Tomb of Painted Basket of Lo-**
lang, 樂浪彩篋塚, Pl. LVI.
Pty of the Author

62 Side table, *ch'iao-t'ou-an;* huang-huali.
Pl 81
Jt 1, 9, 13, 23; Ht of board 81; top, over all,
185 × 41,5.
Pty of Herr J. Plaut

63 Side table, *ch'iao-t'ou-an;* huang-huali.
Pl 82
Jt 1, 9, 13, 21; Ht of board 80,5; top, over all,
158 × 38.
Pty of Oberreichsbahnrat H. J. v. Lochow

64 Bench, *t'iao-teng;* huang-huali.
Measured drawings. Pls 83-85
Jt 1, 13, 21; Ht 48; top 121 × 35; one of a pair.
Pty of the Author

65 Side table, *ch'iao-t'ou-an;* huang-huali.
Pl 86
Jt 1, 9, 13, 21; Ht of board 84; top, over all,
226 × 52.
Pty of Minister E. Boltze, formerly of
Dr. Alfred Hoffmann

66 Side table, *ch'iao-t'ou-an;* chich'ihmu. Pl 87
Jt 1, 9, 13, 21; Ht of board 89; top, over all,
343,5 × 50. Inscription with date, Dec./Jan.
1640/41, incised on the underside of top board,
崇禎庚辰仲冬製於旅署.
Pty of Messrs. Lun-ku-chai 論古齋, Peking

67 Side table, *p'ing-t'ou-an;* huang-huali.
Pl 88
Jt 1, 12, 16, 21; Ht 85; top 162,5 × 51.
Pty of Dr. Mathias Komor

68 Side table, *p'ing-t'ou-an;* bamboo veneer.
Pl 89
Jt 1, 13, 23; Ht 80; top 184 × 43; one of a set
of four.
Pty of Mrs. W. J. Calhoun

69 Trestle table, *chia-chi-an;* huang-huali
stands with lao-huali top.
Pls 90, 159 left bottom
Jt 10, 25; full Ht 64; top 164 × 30.
Pty of the Author

70 Trestle table, *chia-chi-an;* chich'ihmu
(*Ormosia hosiei?*). Pl 91
Jt 10, 25; full Ht 91; top 222 × 38.
Pty of Mme Henri Vetch

71 Separate trestle support (occasional
stand), *chia-chi;* huang-huali. Pl 92
Jt 10, 20; Ht 86, 5; top 41,5 × 41,5.
Pty of Messrs. Robert and William Drummond

72 Stool, *wu-teng;* huang-huali. Pl 94 left
Jt 1, 2, 6, 27; Ht 49, 5; seat, over all, 55 × 46;
one of a pair.
Pty of the Author

73 Stool, *wu-teng;* hungmu. Pls 93, 94 right
Jt 1, 2, 6, 16, 27; Ht 47; seat, over all, 59 × 59;
one of a pair.
Pty of Herr J. Plaut

74 Stool, *wu-teng;* huang-huali.
Measured drawings. Pls 95 left, 96
Jt 11; board-seat; Ht 50; seat 42 × 42; one of
a pair.
Pty of the Author

75 Stool, *wu-teng;* huang-huali. Pl 95 right
Jt 11, 27; Ht 52; seat, over all, 44 × 44; one
of a pair.
Pty of Mme Henri Vetch

76 Stool, *wu-teng;* huang-huali. Pl 97 right
Jt 1, 5, 24, 27; Ht 48; seat, over all, 54 × 54.
Pty of Dr. Derk Bodde

77 Stool, *wu-teng;* huang-huali. Pl 97 left
Jt 1, 5, 24; board-seat; Ht 52, 5; top 74 × 63.
Pty of Messrs. Robert and William Drummond

78 Back chair, *kuan-mao-i;* huang-huali.
Measured drawings. Pls 98, 99
Jt 16, 26, 27; full Ht 111; Ht of seat 52; seat,
over all, 49 × 40; one of a pair.
Pty of the Author

79 Back chair, *kuan-mao-i;* huang-huali.
Measured drawings. Pls 100, 101
Jt 26, 27; full Ht 95; Ht of seat 44; seat, over
all, 51 × 44; one of a pair.
Pty of Miss Faye Whiteside

80 Armchair, *fu-shou-i;* huang-huali. Pl 102
Jt 26, 27; full Ht 120; Ht of seat 51; seat, over all, 58,5 × 46; one of a pair.
Pty of Dr. Alfred Hoffmann

81 Armchair, *fu-shou-i;* huang-huali. Pl 103
Jt 26; board-seat; full Ht 94; Ht of seat 44,5; seat, over all, 56 × 43,5.
Pty of Miss Mabel E. Tom

82 Armchair, *fu-shou-i;* huang-huali. Pl 104
Jt 16, 26, 27; full Ht 100,5; Ht of seat 51; seat, over all, 63 × 50; one of a pair.
Pty of the Author

83 Armchair, *fu-shou-i;* huang-huali.
Pl 105 left
Jt 26, 27; full Ht 105; Ht of seat 50; seat, over all, 65 × 49,5; one of a set of four.
Pty of Prof. Günther Huwer

84 Armchair, *fu-shou-i;* huang-huali.
Pl 105 right
Jt 26, 27; full Ht 105,5; Ht of seat 48; seat, over all, 55 × 43,5; one of a pair.
Pty of Prof. Walter Fuchs

85 Armchair with circular rest, *ch'üan-i;* huang-huali. Pl 106 left
Jt 22, 26, 27; full Ht 88; Ht of seat 48; seat, over all, 59 × 45,5; one of a pair.
Pty of Messrs. Robert and William Drummond

86 Armchair with circular rest, *ch'üan-i;* huang-huali. Pl 106 right
Jt 22, 26, 27; full Ht 99,5; Ht of seat 51; seat, over all, 60 × 47; one of a pair.
Pty of the Author

87 Armchair with circular rest, *ch'üan-i;* huang-huali.
Measured drawings. Pls 107-109
Jt 22, 26, 27; full Ht 102; Ht of seat 52; seat, over all, 62 × 48; one of a pair.
Pty of Gräfin Leonore Lichnowsky and Frau Irene Schierlitz

88 Armchair, *fu-shou-i;* hungmu. Pl 110 left
Jt 26; board-seat; full Ht 91; Ht of seat 51; seat, over all, 66 × 50; one of a pair.
Pty of Harold Acton, Esq.

89 Armchair, *fu-shou-i;* huang-huali.
Pl 110 right
Jt 26, 27; full Ht 82; Ht of seat 49; seat, over all, 62 × 41; one of a pair.
Pty of Oberreichsbahnrat H. J. v. Lochow

90 Cabinet, *shu-kuei;* huang-huali. Pl 111
Jt 1, 8, 11, 17; Ht 189; top 98 × 53; one of a pair.
Pty of H. E. the Italian Ambassador and the Marchesa Taliani de Marchio

91 Cabinet, *shu-kuei;* huang-huali.
Pls 112, 158 left bottom
Jt 1, 8, 11, 17; Ht 172; top 99 × 54; one of a pair.
Pty of Frau Irene Schierlitz

92 Cabinet, *shu-kuei;* huang-huali; details only. Pl 113
Ht of feet, including apron, 28; Ht of lock-plates 30; one of a pair.
Pty of Messrs. Robert and William Drummond

93 Cabinet, *shu-kuei;* huang-huali. Pl 114 left
Jt 1, 8, 11, 17; Ht 153; top 74 × 40; one of a pair.
Pty of Messrs. Robert and William Drummond

94 Cabinet, *shu-kuei;* huang-huali with burl-wood panels.
Measured drawings. Pls 114 right-116
Jt 1, 8, 11, 17; Ht 125; top 75 × 45; one of a pair.
Pty of the Author

95 Cabinet, *shu-kuei;* Persian pine (*Persea nanmu*) with burl-wood panels.
Pl 117 left
Jt 1, 8, 11, 17; Ht 181,5; top 96,5 × 54; one of a pair, with door swung open to show inner arrangement.
Pty of Dr. Karl Gruber

96 Cabinet, *shu-kuei;* Persian pine with burl-wood panels. Pl 117 right
Jt 1, 8, 11, 17; Ht 186; top 100,5 × 54; one of a pair.
Pty of Mme Henri Vetch

97 High-standing coffer, *men-hu-ch'u;* huang-huali. Measured drawings. Pls 118-120
Jt 1, 9, 23, 24; Ht of top board 90; top, over all, 170 × 57.
Pty of the Author

98 High-standing coffer, *men-hu-ch'u;* huang-huali. Pl 121
Jt 1, 9, 23, 24; Ht of top board 83; top, over all, 190 × 62.
Pty of Dr. Mathias Komor

99 Low cupboard with drawers, *lien-erh-ch'u;* huang-huali. Pl 122 bottom
Jt 1, 9, 23, 32; Ht of top board 85; top, over all, 139 × 49.
Pty of Messrs. Robert and William Drummond

100 Low cupboard with drawers, *kuei-ch'u;* huang-huali.
Measured drawings. Pls 122-124, 156, 157
Jt 1, 29-32; Ht 86; top 128 × 54.
Pty of the Author

101 Compound wardrobe in four parts, *ssu-chien-kuei,* huang-huali.
Pls 125, 156, 157
Jt 1, 29-32, 34; Ht of principal piece 180,5; of upper piece 80; top of single piece 104,5 × 54,5.
Pty of Mme Henri Vetch

102 Compound wardrobe in two parts, *ting-shu-kuei;* huang-huali. Pls 126, 157
Jt 1, 29-32, 34; Ht of principal piece 206,5; of upper piece 74; top 172,5 × 71; one of a pair.
Pty of Prof. Günther Huwer

103 Compound wardrobe in two parts, *ting-shu-kuei;* huang-huali.
Measured drawings. Pls 127-130, 158, 159
Jt 1, 29-34; Ht of principal piece 185; of upper piece 92; top 142 × 71; one of a pair.
Pty of H. E. Baron Jules Guillaume and the Author. A similar set in the possession of M. L. de Hessel

104 Cabinet, *shu-kuei;* huang-huali.　　Pl 131
　　Jt 1, 29-32, 34; Ht 198,5; top 115 × 51; one of
　　a pair.
　　　　　Pty of Messrs. Robert and William Drummond

105 Cabinet, *shu-kuei;* huang-huali.
　　Measured drawings. Pls 132, 133, 156, 158
　　Jt 1, 29-32, 34; Ht 160; top 82 × 47; one of a
　　pair.
　　　　　　　　　　　　　　　Pty of the Author

106 Compound cabinet in two parts, *ch'u-kuei;*
　　huang-huali.　　　　　　　　　Pl 134
　　Jt 1, 29-32, 34; Ht of principal piece 86,5; of
　　upper piece 68,5; top of principal piece 73 × 58;
　　of upper piece 69,5 × 54,5.
　　　　　　　　　　　Pty of M. Jean Pierre Dubosc

107 Medicine cabinet, *yao-ch'u;* huang-huali.
　　　　　　　　　　　　　　　　　Pl 135
　　Jt 1, 15, 29-31; Ht 58; top 55 × 35; the bottom
　　picture shows the cabinet open, with nest of
　　drawers and central recess for Buddhist image.
　　　　　　　　　　　Pty of Dr. R. J. C. Hoeppli

108 Medicine cabinet, *yao-ch'u;* huang-huali.
　　Pls 136 top, 159 left top (enlarged), 160
　　Jt 1, 15, 29-31; Ht 33; top 31 × 22,5.
　　　　　　Pty of Prof. Yang Tsung-han 楊宗翰

109 Medicine box, *yao-hsiang;* huang-huali.
　　　　　　　　　　　　　　Pl 136 bottom
　　Jt 1, 15, dovetails; Ht 39; top 37,5 × 31; one
　　of a pair.
　　　　　　Pty of Gräfin Leonore Lichnowsky and
　　　　　　　　　　　　　　　Dr. Beate Krieg

110 Circular stand with three legs, *san-chiao
　　yüan-chi;* huang-huali.
　　　　　　Measured drawings. Pls 137, 138
　　Jt 1, 4, 20, 22; full Ht 87; diameter of top 47,5.
　　　　　　Pty of Miss Tseng Yu-ho 曾幼荷.

111 Circular stand with five legs, *wu-chiao
　　yüan-chi;* Persian pine.　　Pls 139, 140
　　Jt 1, 4; full Ht 91; diameter of top 38.
　　　　　　　　　Pty of Prof. Günther Huwer

112 Circular stand (seat) in form of a melon,
　　kua-leng-tun; huang-huali.　　Pl 141 left
　　Jt 1; Ht 41; diameter of top 26.
　　　　　　　　　　　　　Pty of the Author

113 Circular stand (seat) in form of a drum,
　　ku-erh-tun; hungmu.　　　　Pl 141 right
　　Jt 1, 4; Ht 51,5; diameter of top 37,5.
　　　　　　　　　Pty of Dr. R. J. C. Hoeppli

114 Stands for candle with lantern, *chu-t'ai;*
115 114 tzut'an; 115, 116 huang-huali. Pl 142
116 114, Ht 149.　　　　Pty of Mme Henri Vetch
　　　115, Ht, not extended, 126.　Pty of the Author
　　　116, Ht 163,5.　　　　　　　Pty of the Author
　　　Measurements without lanterns

117 Wash-stands, *p'en-chia;* huang-huali.
118 　　　　　　　Pls 143, 144, 148-151
119 117, Ht of top rail 170.　Pty of the Author
　　　118, Ht of top rail 180.　Pty of the Author
　　　119, Ht of top rail 167,5.
　　　　　　　　　　Pty of Mme Henri Vetch

120 Stand for flower-pot or wash-basin, *chia-
　　tzu;* huang-huali.　　　　　　Pl 145
　　Full Ht 70.　　　Pty of Herr Hans Wechsel

121 Clothes-rack, *i-chia;* huang-huali.　Pl 146
　　Ht of top rail 166,5; top, over all, 175,5; width
　　of feet 55,5.
　　　　　　　　　　Pty of Mme Henri Vetch

122 Clothes-rack, *i-chia;* huang-huali.
　　　　　　　　　　Pls 147, 149, 150
　　Ht of top rail 168,5; top, over all, 176; width
　　of feet 47,5.
　　　　　　　　　　　　　Pty of the Author

中國花梨家具圖攷

著作者　艾克

出版者　魏智

印刷者　北京　〔珂羅版〕彩華印刷局　輔仁大學印書局　遣使會印書館

發行者　北京　法文圖書館

中華民國三十三年十月

Original Chinese colophon

THE PLATES

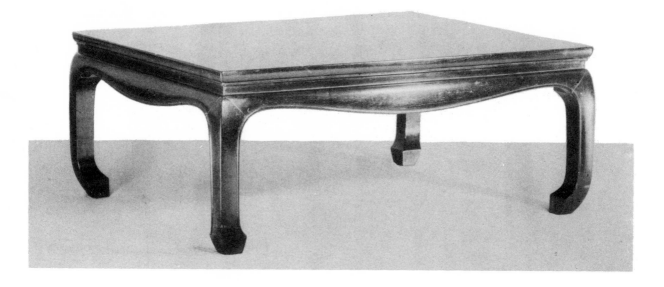

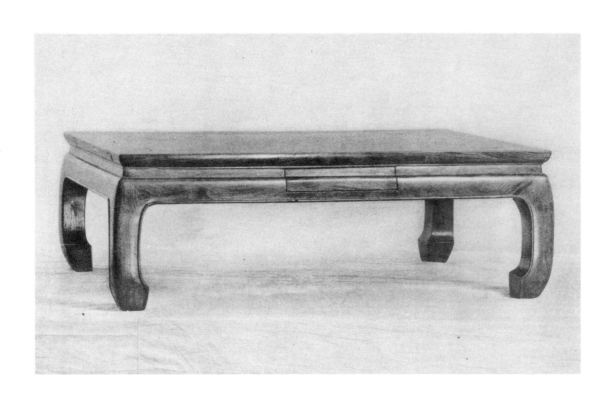

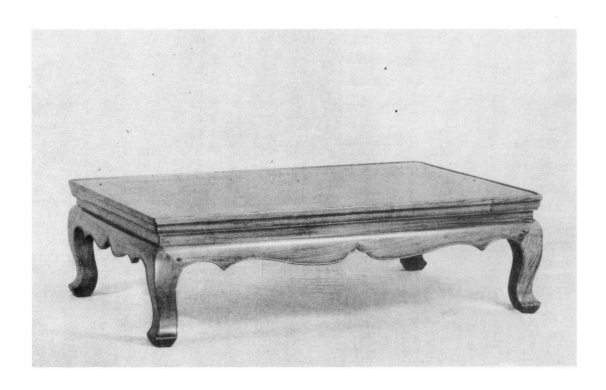

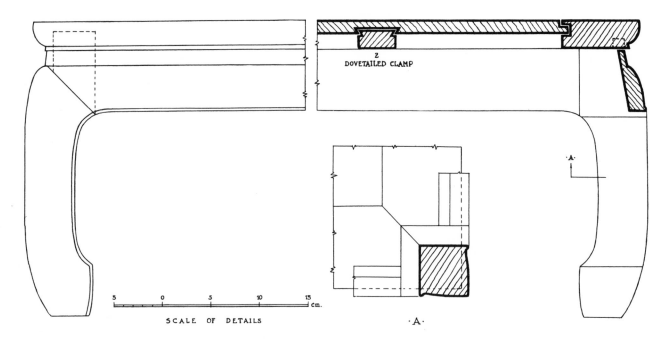

DOVETAILED CLAMP

·A·

5   0   5   10   15
Cm.

SCALE OF DETAILS

·A·

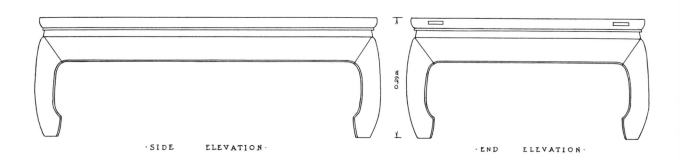

·SIDE   ELEVATION·

·END   ELEVATION·

0.29 m

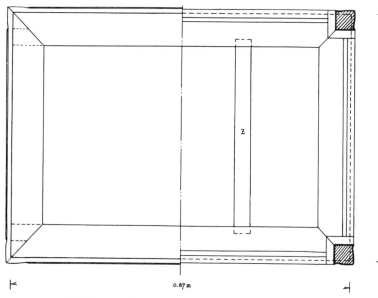

Z

0.60 m

0.87 m

·PLAN OF TOP·   ·PLAN LOOKING UP·

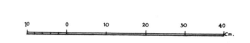

10   0   10   20   30   40
Cm.

COUCH TABLE

G. ECKE DIREX.   Y. YANG DELIN.
1936
IN THE POSSESSION OF L. C. S. SICKMAN, ESQ.

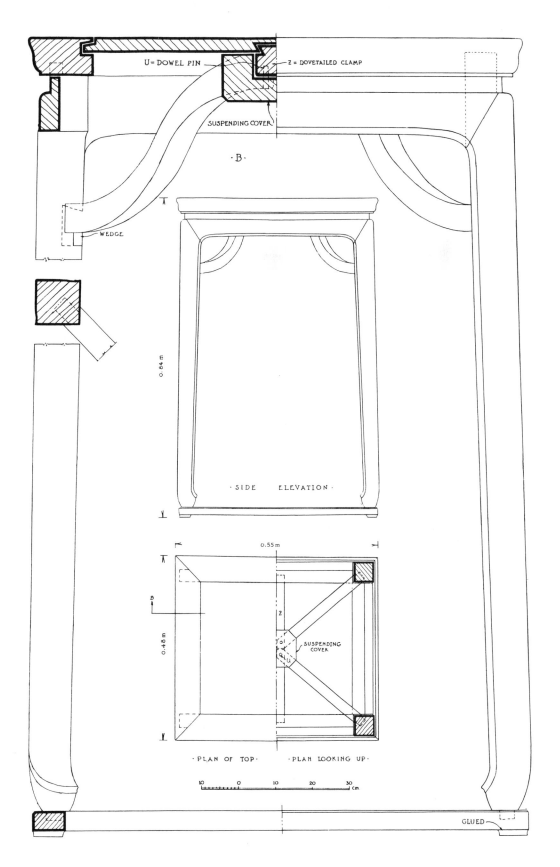

U = DOWEL PIN   Z = DOVETAILED CLAMP

SUSPENDING COVER

·B·

WEDGE

0.84 m

·SIDE ELEVATION·

0.55 m

B

Z

0.48 m

SUSPENDING COVER

·PLAN OF TOP·   ·PLAN LOOKING UP·

GLUED

TEA TABLE

G. ECKE Direx.   Y. YANG Delin.

1938

SCALE OF DETAILS

IN THE POSSESSION OF A. L. POLLARD-URQUHART, Esq.

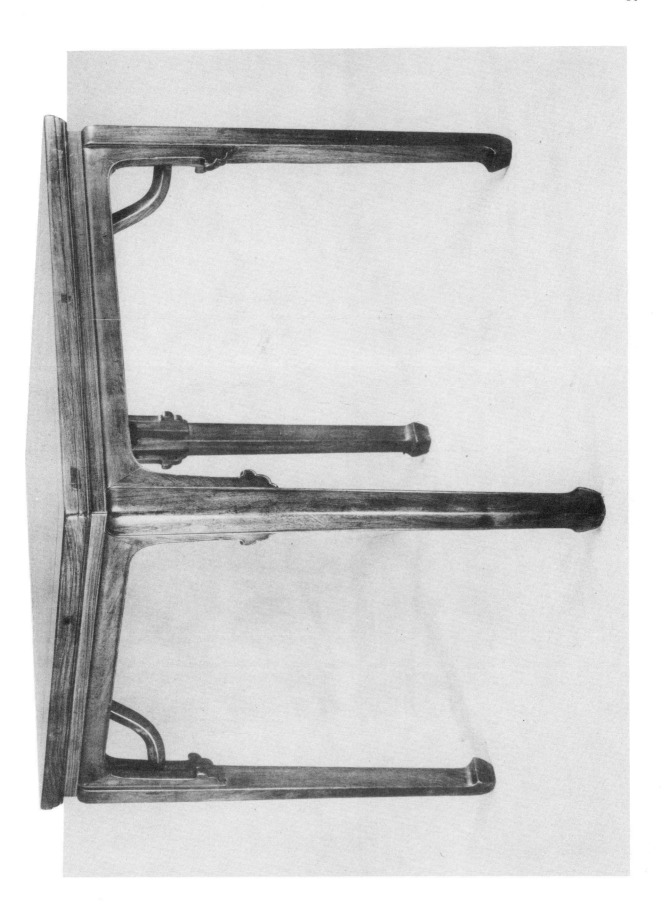

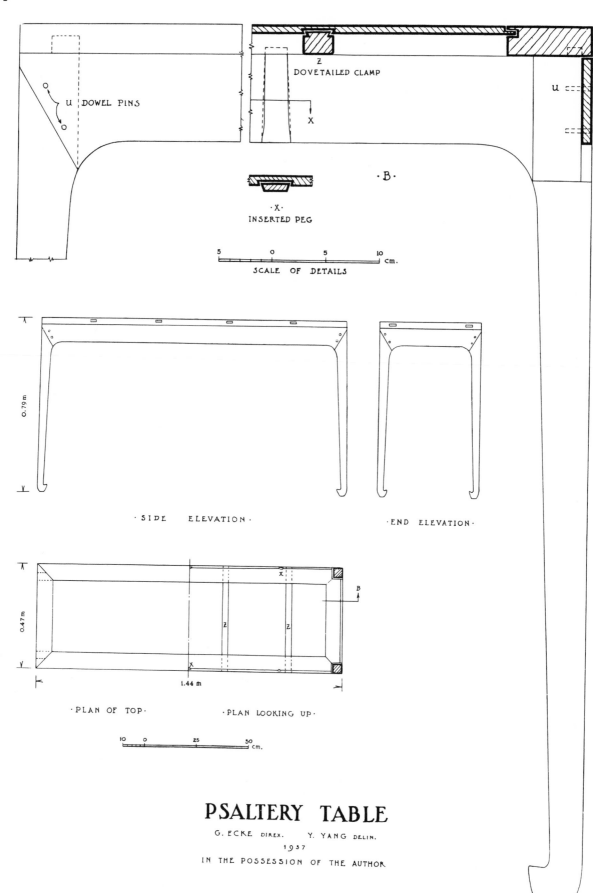

U DOWEL PINS

Z
DOVETAILED CLAMP

X

·B·

U

·X·
INSERTED PEG

5   0   5   10 Cm.
SCALE OF DETAILS

0.79 m

·SIDE   ELEVATION·

·END ELEVATION·

0.47 m

B

Z   Z

X

1.44 m

·PLAN OF TOP·   ·PLAN LOOKING UP·

10   0   25   50 Cm.

PSALTERY TABLE
G. ECKE DIREX.   Y. YANG DELIN.
1937
IN THE POSSESSION OF THE AUTHOR

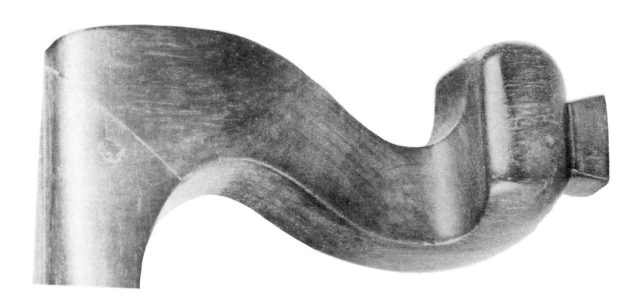

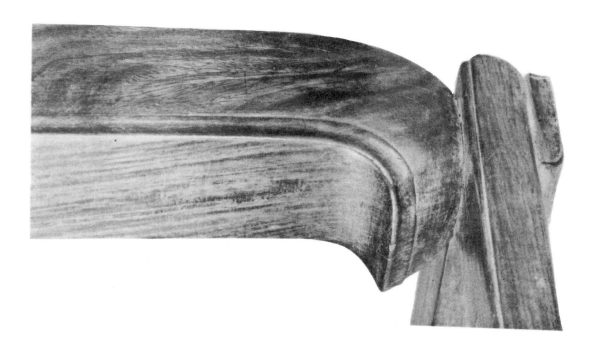

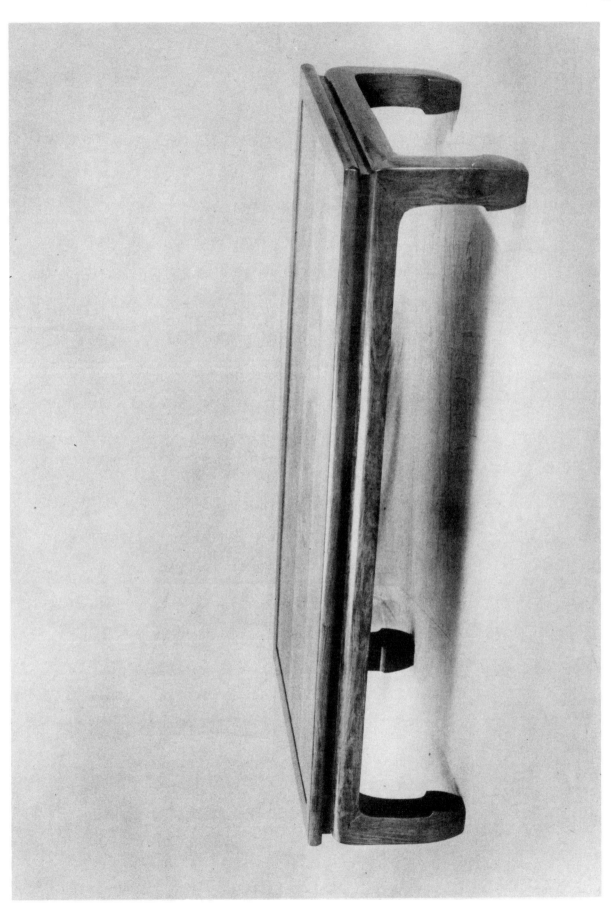

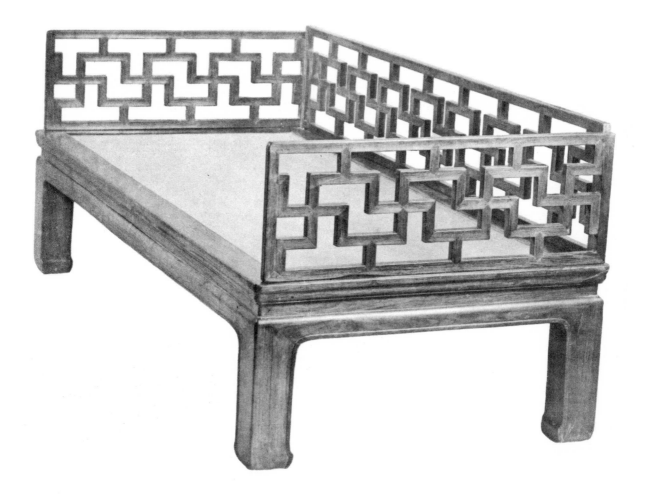

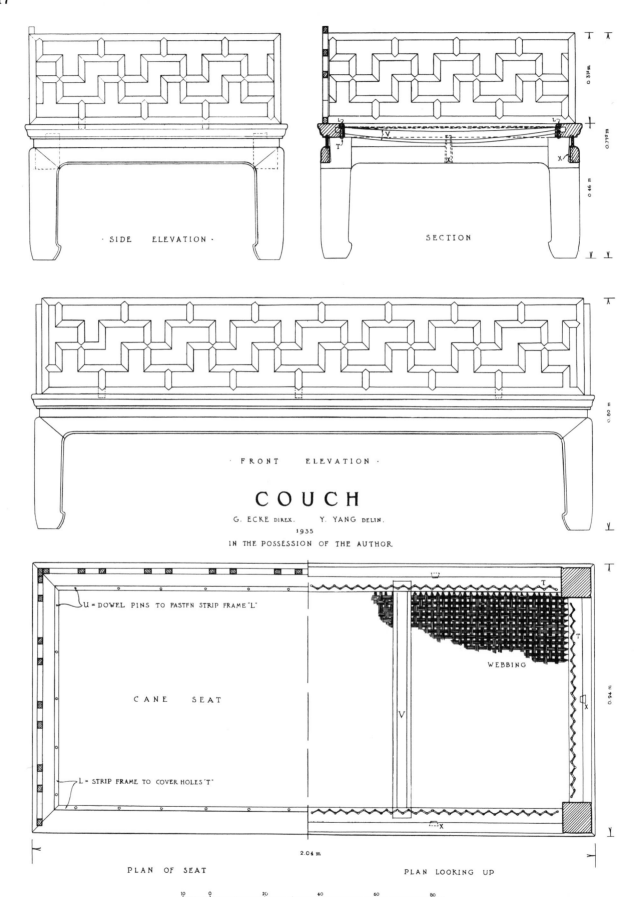

· SIDE ELEVATION ·

SECTION

· FRONT ELEVATION ·

COUCH

G. ECKE DIREX.   Y. YANG DELIN.

1935

IN THE POSSESSION OF THE AUTHOR

U = DOWEL PINS TO FASTEN STRIP FRAME "L"

CANE SEAT

WEBBING

L = STRIP FRAME TO COVER HOLES "T"

PLAN OF SEAT

PLAN LOOKING UP

2.04 m

10   0   20   40   60   80
                                    CM.

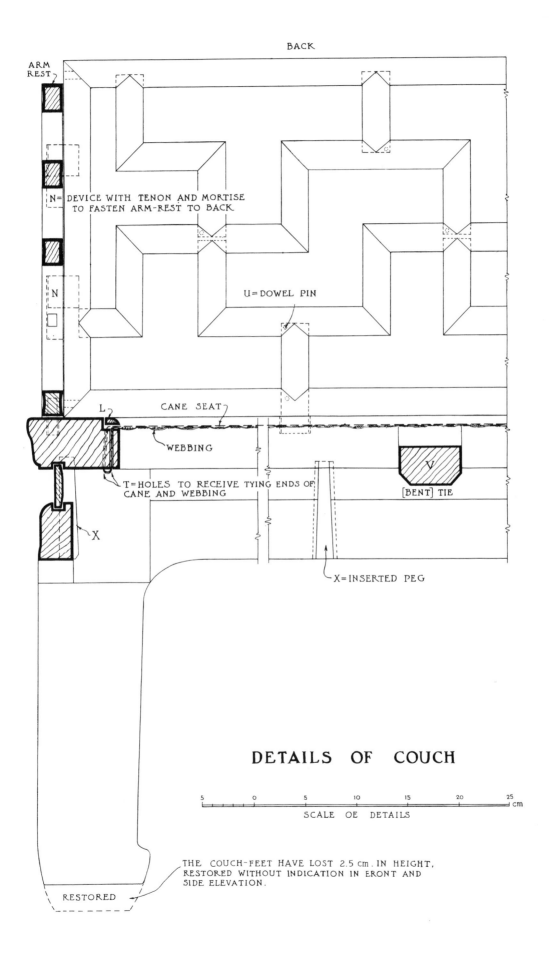

BACK

ARM
REST

N= DEVICE WITH TENON AND MORTISE
TO FASTEN ARM-REST TO BACK.

N

U= DOWEL PIN

L

CANE SEAT

WEBBING

V

T= HOLES TO RECEIVE TYING ENDS OF
CANE AND WEBBING

[BENT] TIE

X

X= INSERTED PEG

DETAILS OF COUCH

SCALE OE DETAILS

THE COUCH-FEET HAVE LOST 2.5 cm. IN HEIGHT,
RESTORED WITHOUT INDICATION IN FRONT AND
SIDE ELEVATION.

RESTORED

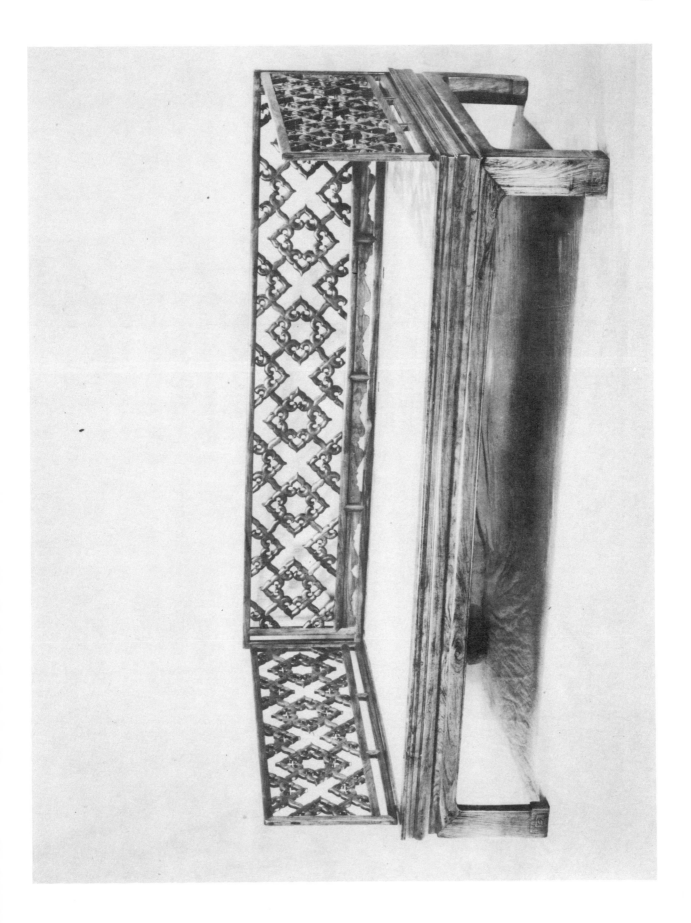

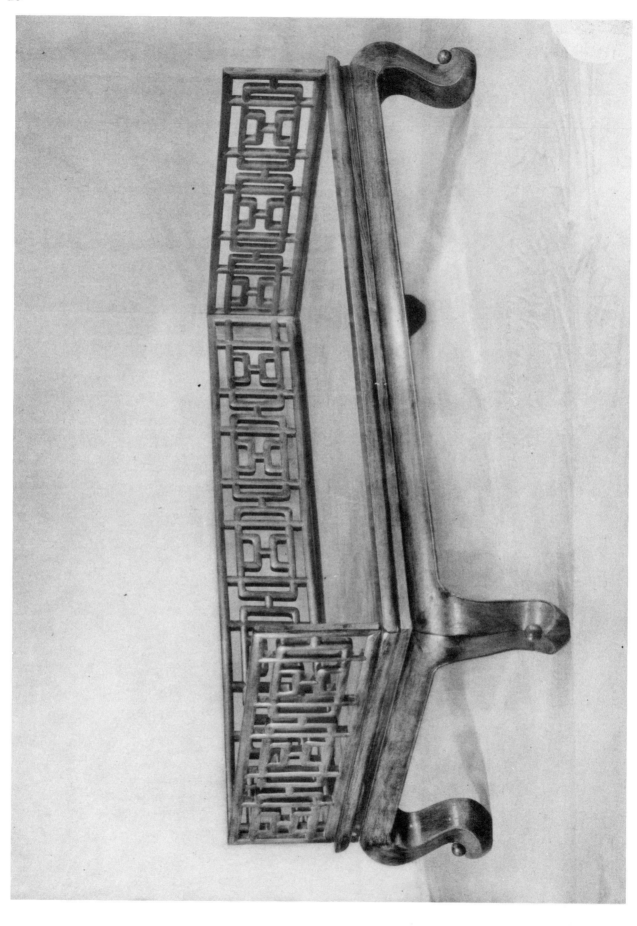

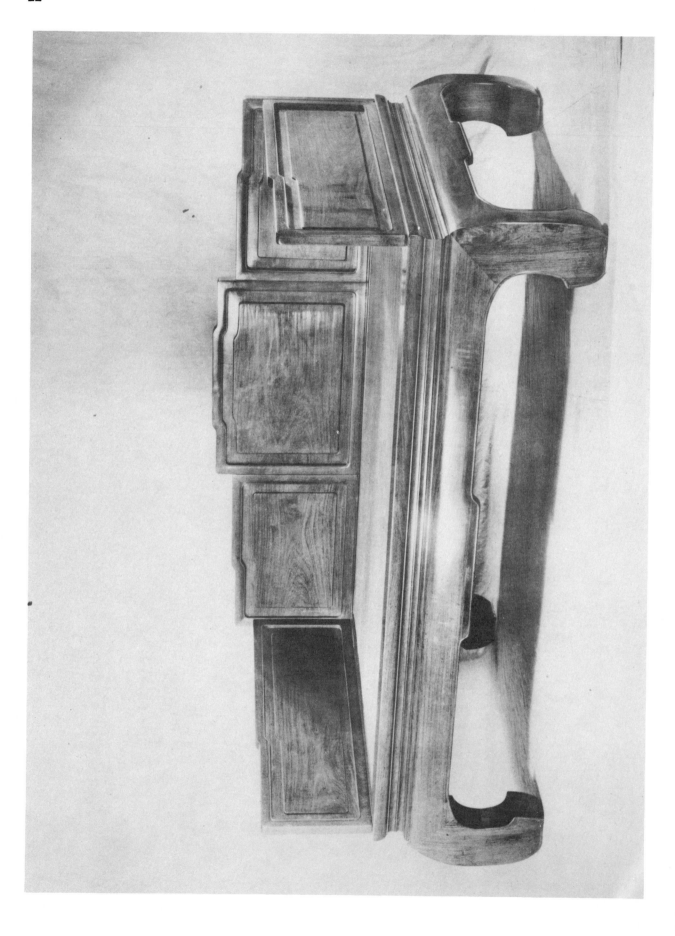

· FRONT   ELEVATION ·

BEDSTEAD

G. ECKE DIREX   Y. YANG DELIN.

1937

IN THE POSSESSION OF THE AUTHOR

2.42 m

· SIDE   ELEVATION ·

BEDSTEAD
[CONTINUED]

10 0   20   40   60 cm

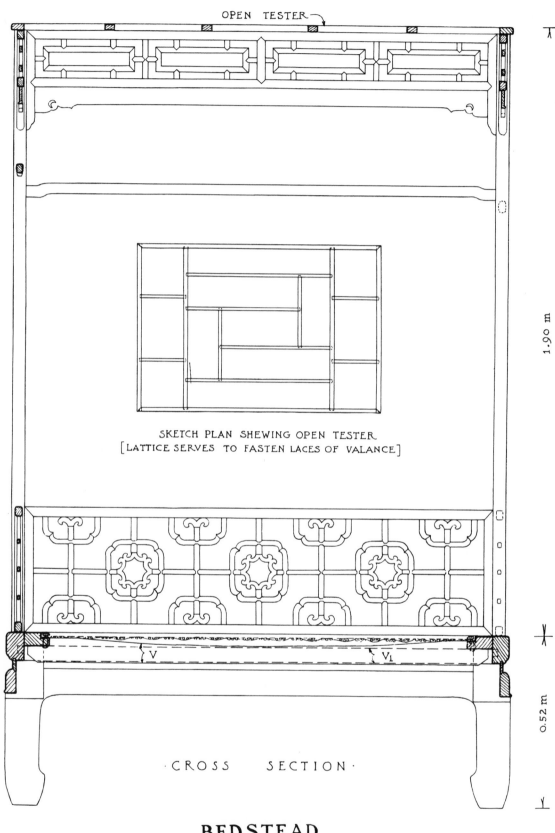

OPEN TESTER

SKETCH PLAN SHEWING OPEN TESTER
[LATTICE SERVES TO FASTEN LACES OF VALANCE]

V   V₁

· CROSS   SECTION ·

1·90 m

0.52 m

BEDSTEAD
[CONTINUED]

10   0   20   40   60 cm

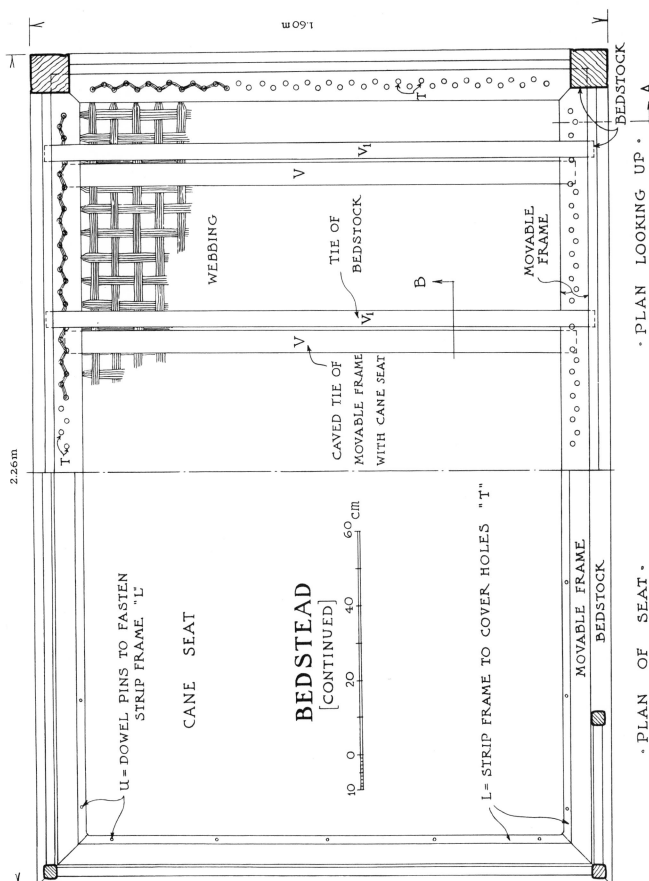

1.60 m

2.26m

BEDSTOCK

⌐A

· PLAN LOOKING UP ·

V₁

V

TIE OF
BEDSTOCK

MOVABLE
FRAME

B

V₁

WEBBING

V

T

CAVED TIE OF
MOVABLE FRAME
WITH CANE SEAT

T

U = DOWEL PINS TO FASTEN
STRIP FRAME "L"

CANE   SEAT

BEDSTEAD
[CONTINUED]

10   0   20   40   60 cm

L = STRIP FRAME TO COVER HOLES "T"

MOVABLE FRAME

BEDSTOCK

· PLAN   OF   SEAT ·

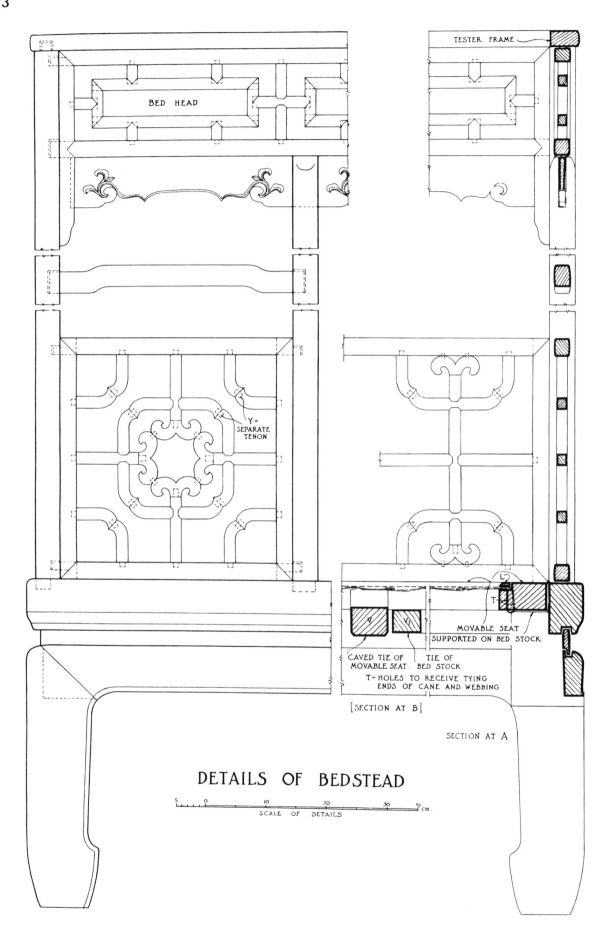

TESTER FRAME

BED HEAD

Y =
SEPARATE
TENON

MOVABLE SEAT
SUPPORTED ON BED STOCK

CAVED TIE OF   TIE OF
MOVABLE SEAT.   BED STOCK

T= HOLES TO RECEIVE TYING
ENDS OF CANE AND WEBBING

[SECTION AT B]

SECTION AT A

DETAILS OF BEDSTEAD

SCALE OF DETAILS

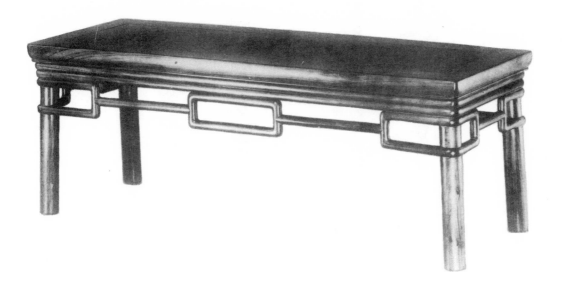

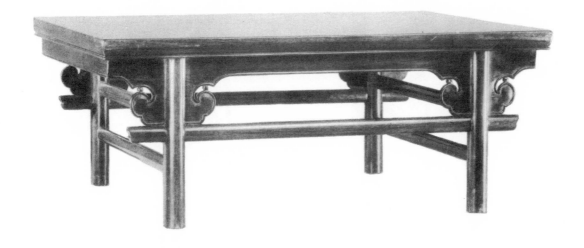

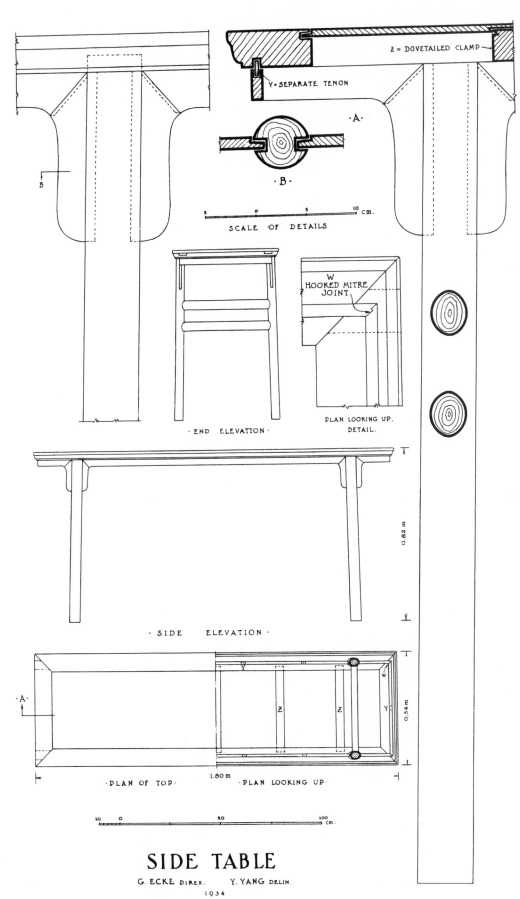

Z = DOVETAILED CLAMP

Y = SEPARATE TENON

·A·

·B·

5   0   5   10   CM.

SCALE OF DETAILS

W
HOOKED MITRE
JOINT

· END ELEVATION ·

PLAN LOOKING UP,
DETAIL.

· SIDE   ELEVATION ·

0.82 m

·A·

0.54 m

· PLAN OF TOP ·   · PLAN LOOKING UP ·

1.80 m

10   0   50   100
CM.

SIDE TABLE

G. ECKE DIREX.   Y. YANG DELIN.

1934

IN THE POSSESSION OF DR. R. J. C. HOEPPLI

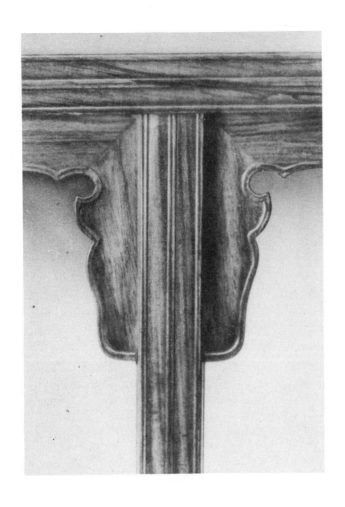

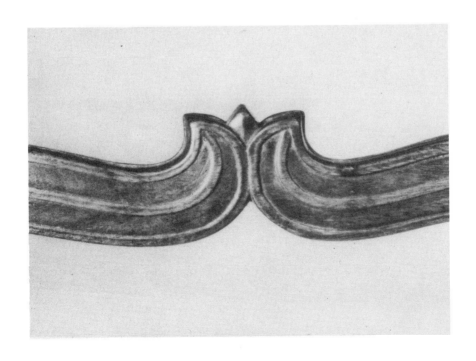

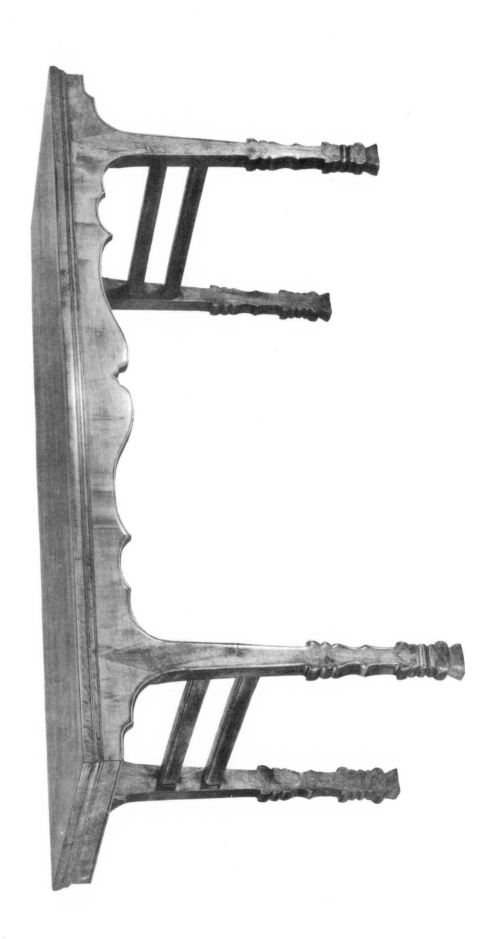

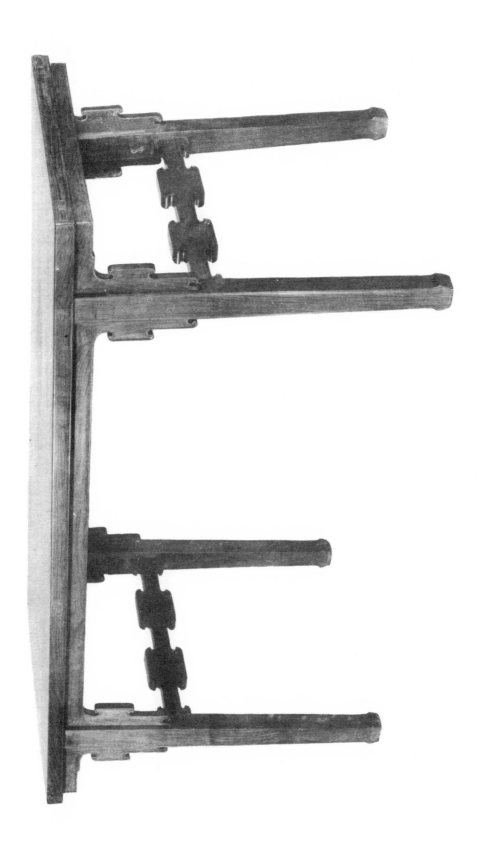

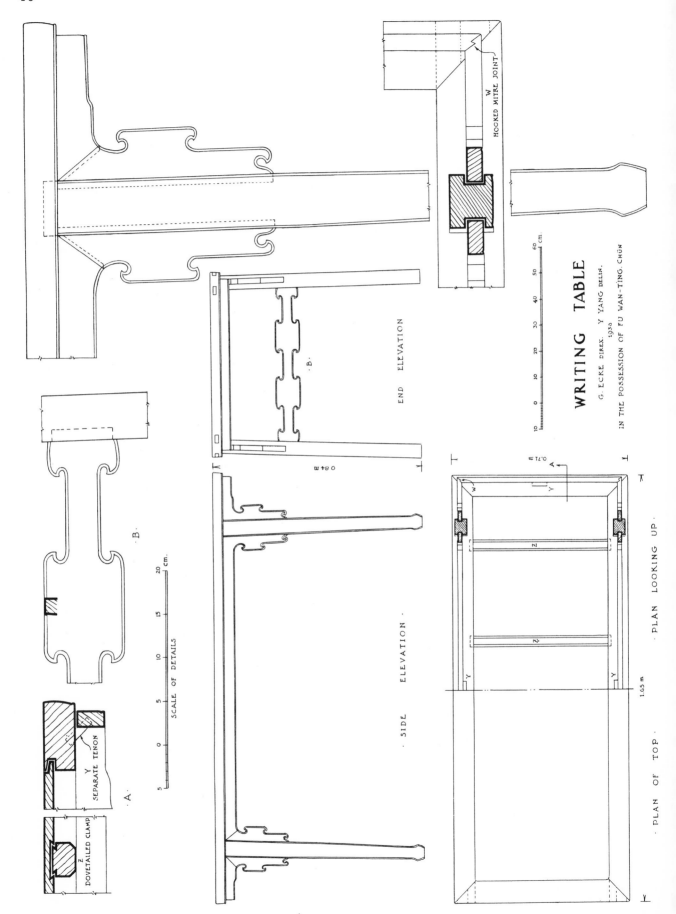

HOOKED MITRE JOINT

END ELEVATION

0.84 m

WRITING TABLE

G. ECKE DIREX. Y YANG DELIN.
1930

IN THE POSSESSION OF FU WAN-TING CHÜN

SCALE OF DETAILS

20 cm.

15

10

5

0

5

·B·

·B·

·A·

SEPARATE TENON

DOVETAILED CLAMP

·SIDE ELEVATION·

0.71 m

·PLAN LOOKING UP·

1.65 m

·PLAN OF TOP·

41

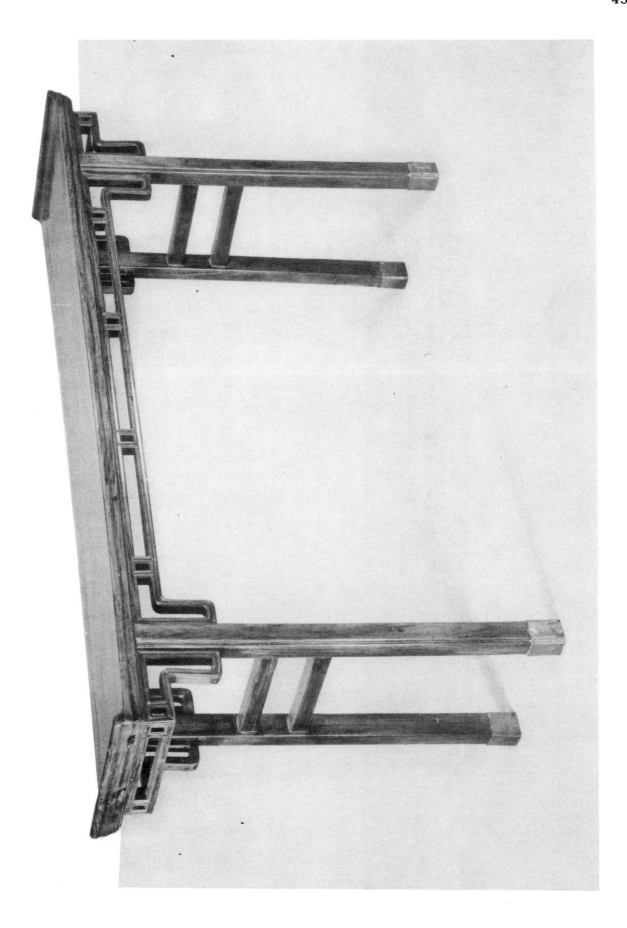

44

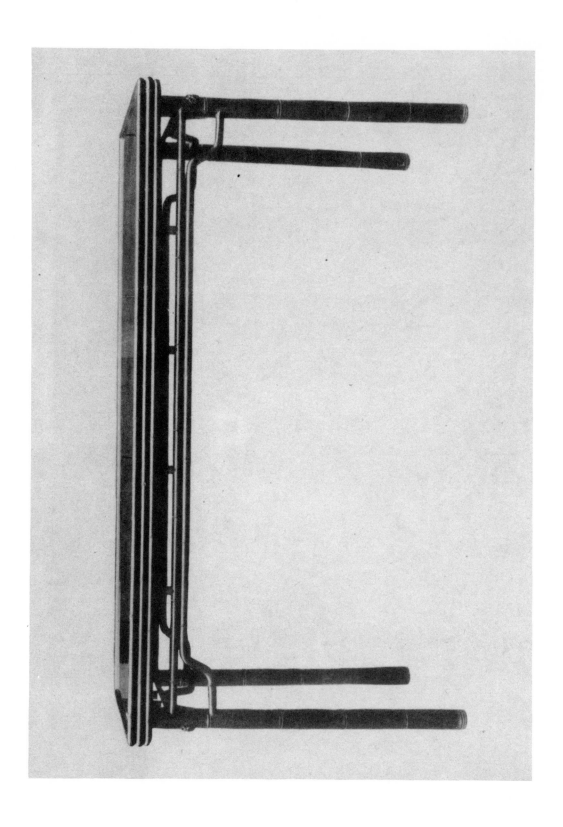

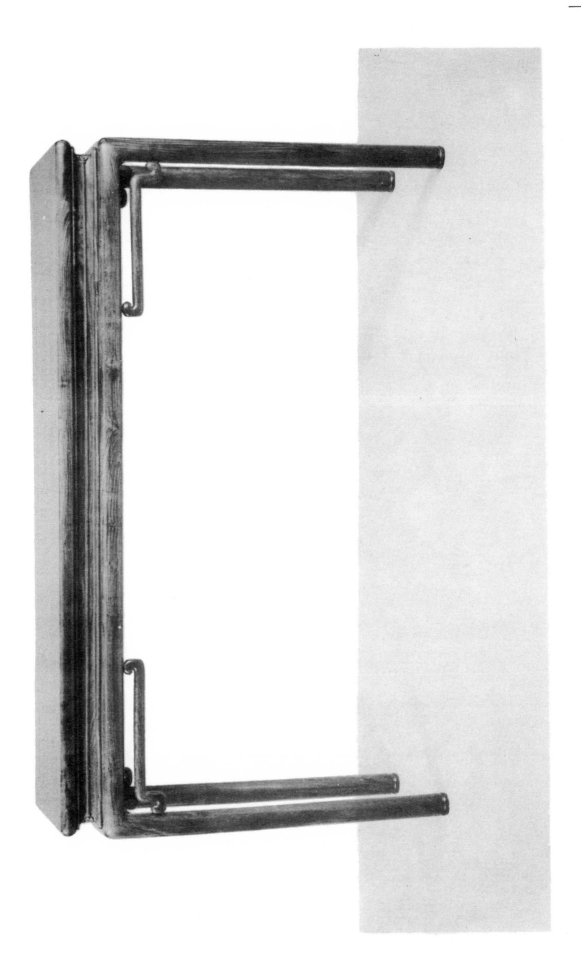

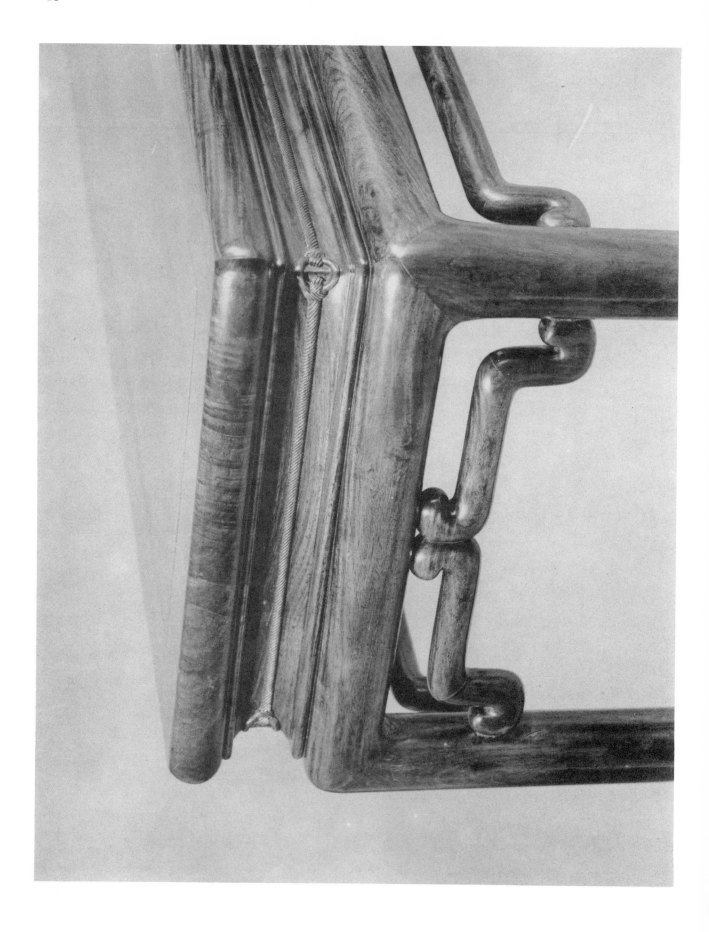

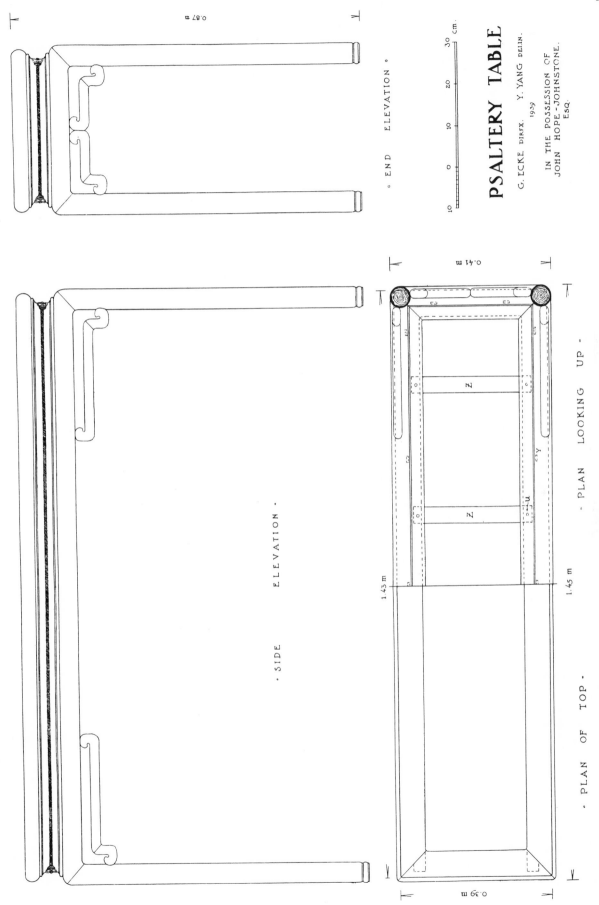

END ELEVATION.

0.87 m

PSALTERY TABLE

G. ECKE DIRKX.   Y. YANG DELIN.
1939

IN THE POSSESSION OF
JOHN HOPE-JOHNSTONE.
ESQ.

30 cm.
20
10
0
10

SIDE ELEVATION.

PLAN OF TOP.

PLAN LOOKING UP.

0.41 m

1.43 m

1.45 m

0.39 m

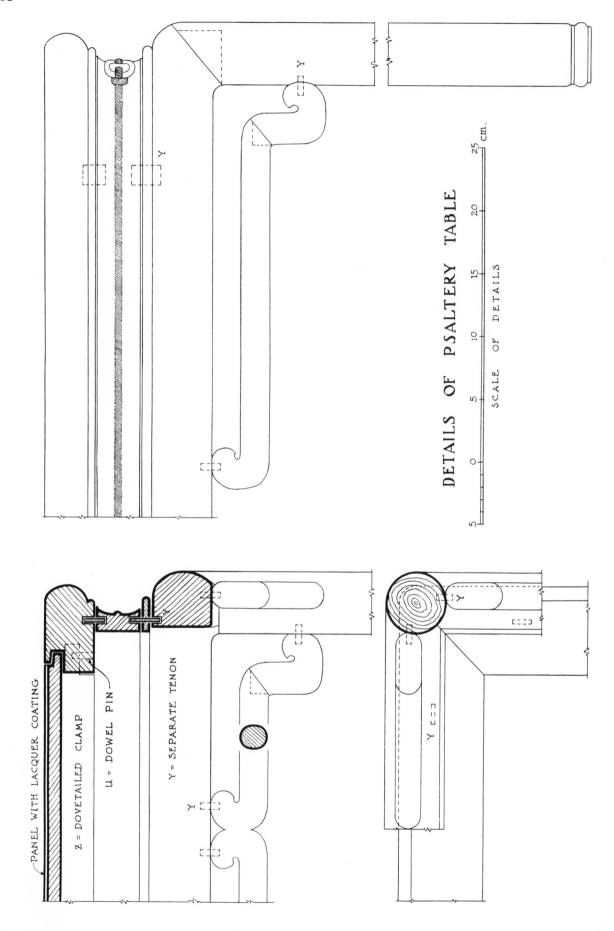

DETAILS OF PSALTERY TABLE

SCALE OF DETAILS

PANEL WITH LACQUER COATING

Z = DOVETAILED CLAMP

U = DOWEL PIN

Y = SEPARATE TENON

51

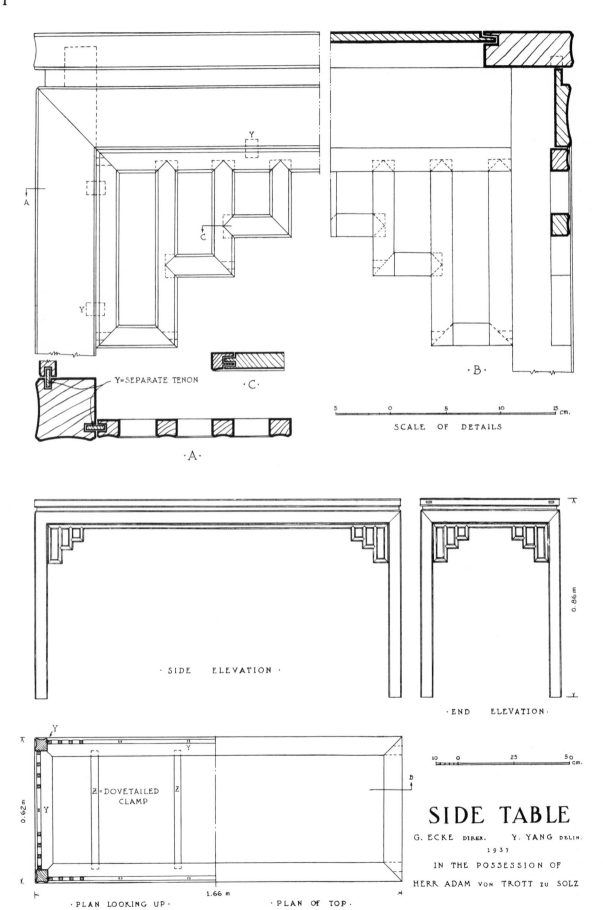

Y=SEPARATE TENON

·C·

·A·

·B·

5   0   5   10   15 cm.

SCALE OF DETAILS

· SIDE   ELEVATION ·

· END   ELEVATION ·

0.86 m

Z=DOVETAILED
CLAMP

0.62 m

1.66 m

·PLAN LOOKING UP·   ·PLAN OF TOP·

10   0   25   50 cm.

SIDE TABLE

G. ECKE DIREX.   Y. YANG DELIN.

1937

IN THE POSSESSION OF

HERR ADAM VON TROTT ZU SOLZ

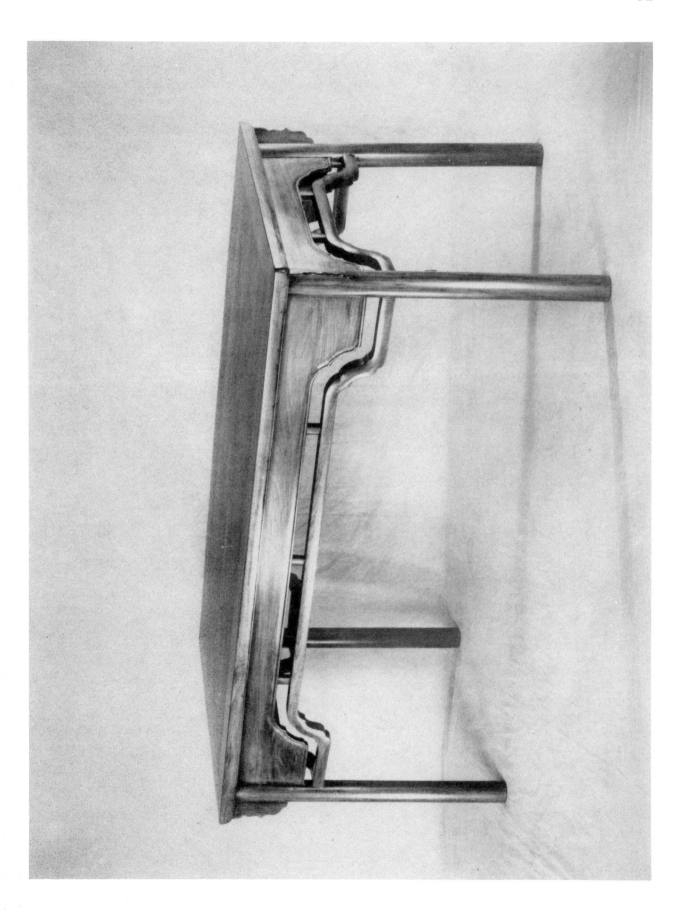

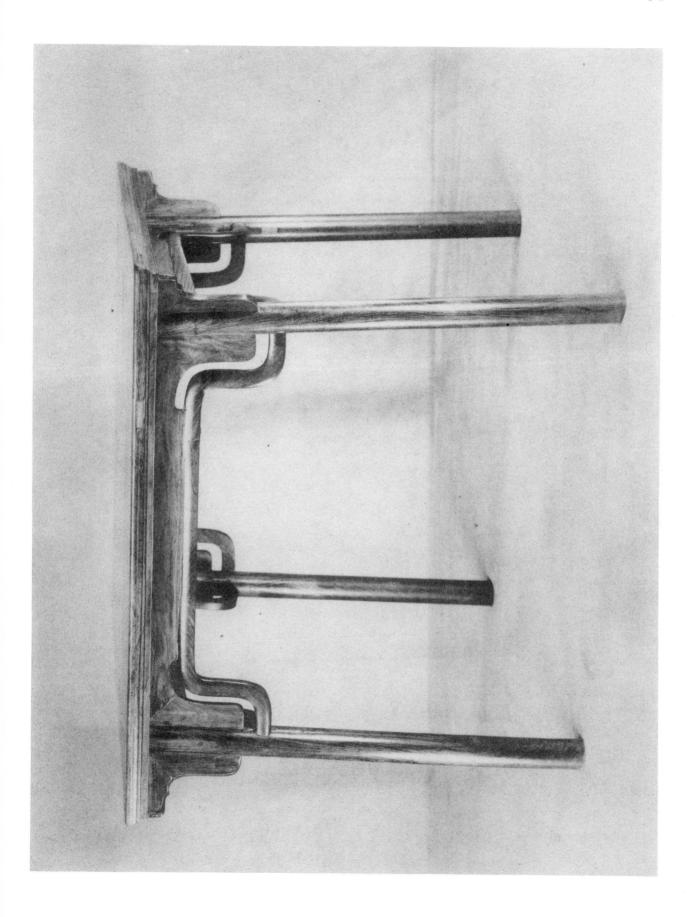

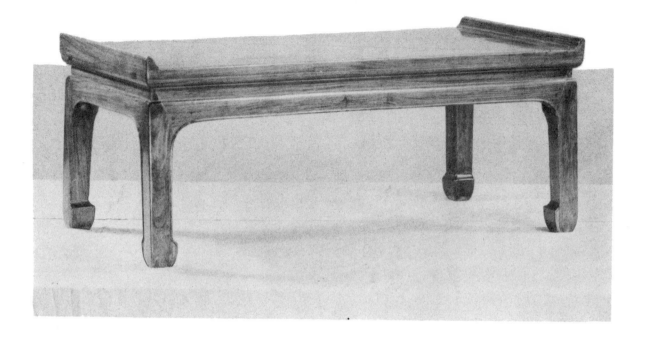

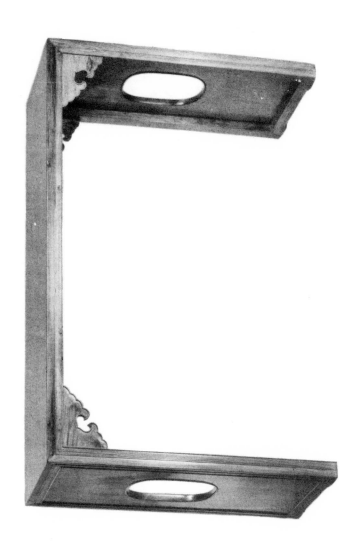

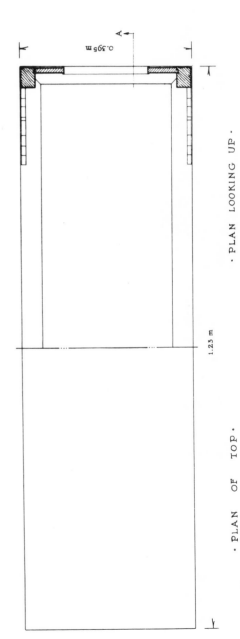

60

· END ELEVATION ·

0.795 m

PSALTERY TABLE

G. ECKE DIREX.   Y. YANG DELIN.
1939

IN THE POSSESSION OF
MESSRS ROBERT AND WILLIAM DRUMMOND

cm.

10   0   10   20   30

· SIDE   ELEVATION ·

· PLAN   OF   TOP ·

0.395 m

1.23 m

· PLAN LOOKING UP ·

A

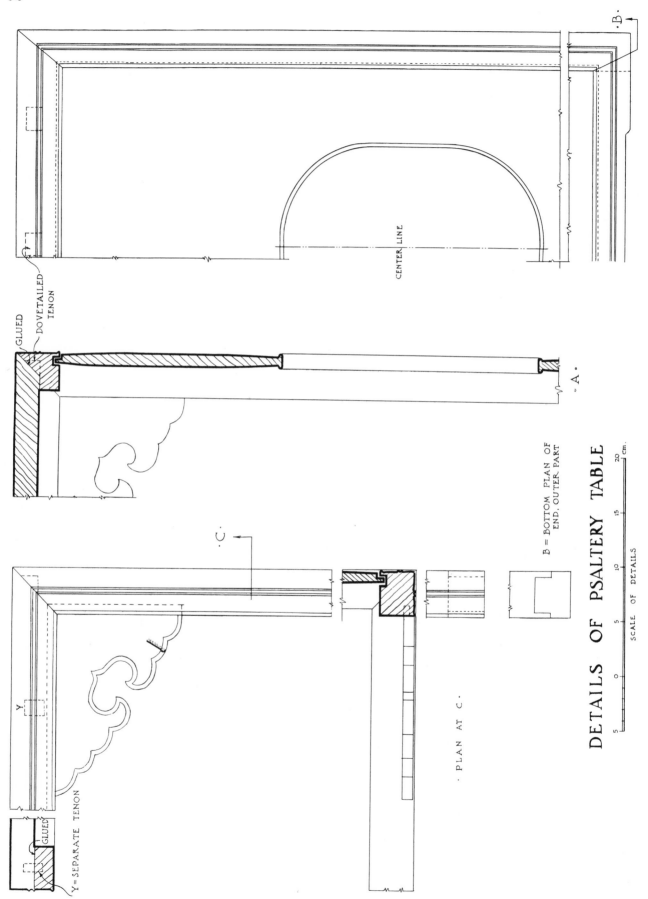

78

CENTER LINE

GLUED

DOVETAILED
TENON

·A·

·B·

Y

Y = SEPARATE TENON

GLUED

·C·

B = BOTTOM PLAN OF
END. OUTER PART

·PLAN AT C·

DETAILS OF PSALTERY TABLE

SCALE OF DETAILS

5   0   5   10   15   20 cm.

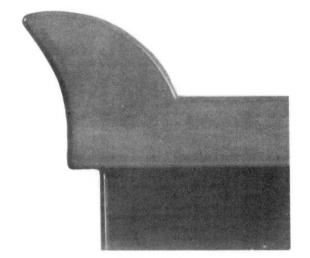
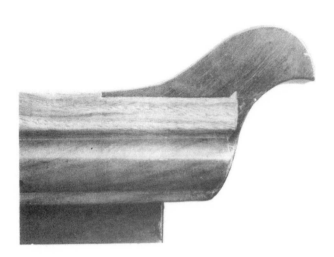

61

63

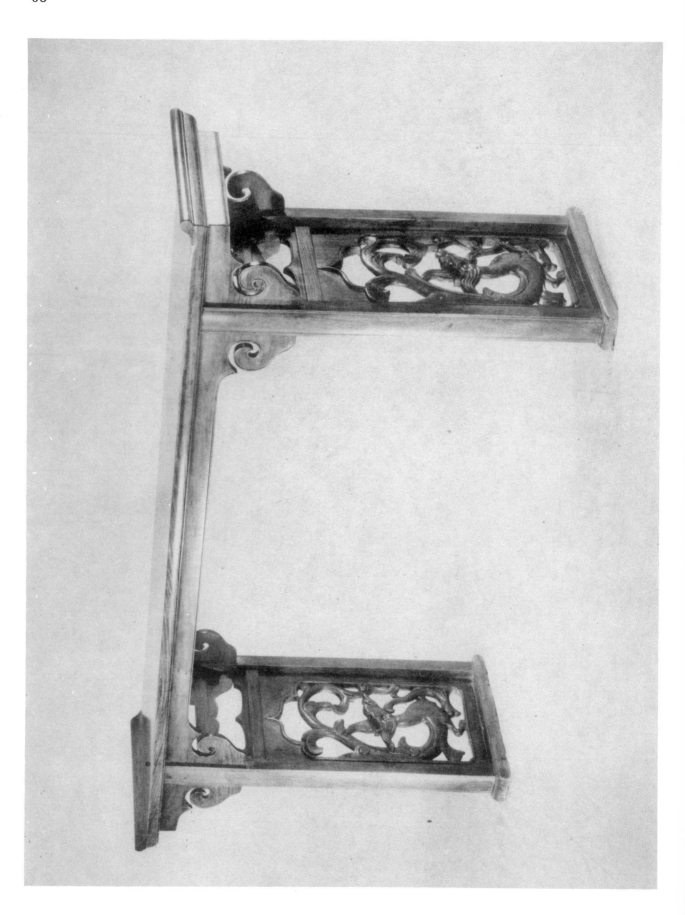

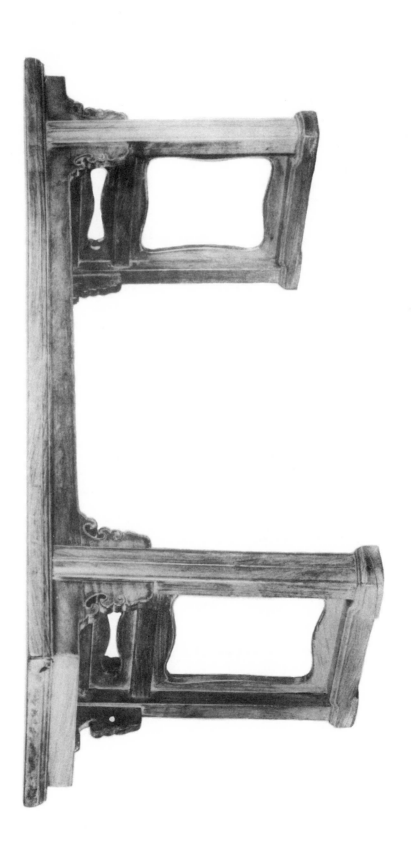

64

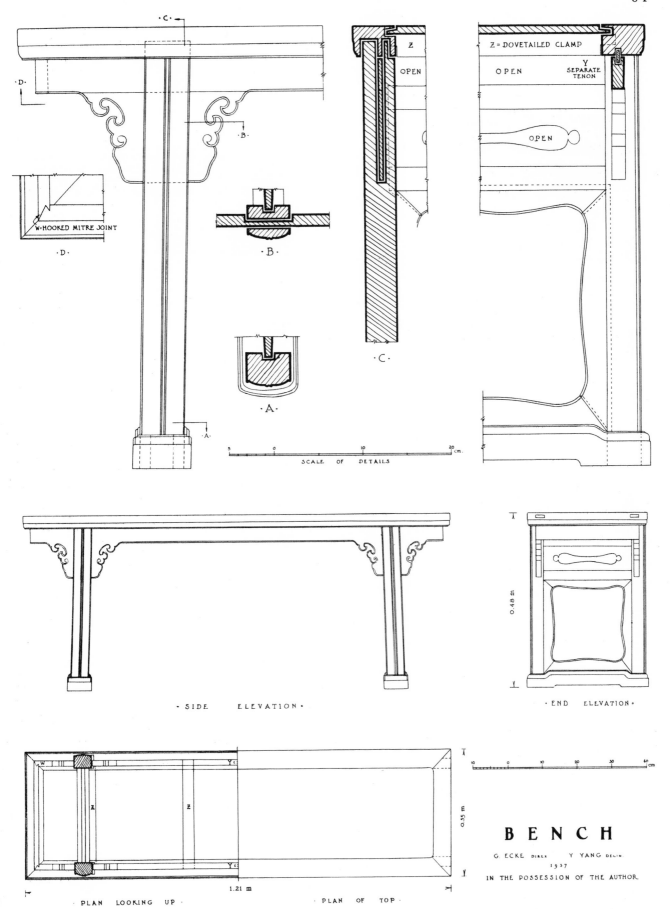

·C·

·D·

·B·

W·HOOKED MITRE JOINT

·D·

·B·

·A·

Z

OPEN

·C·

Z = DOVETAILED CLAMP

OPEN

Y
SEPARATE
TENON

OPEN

SCALE   OF   DETAILS

5   0   10   20   cm.

· SIDE   ELEVATION ·

· END   ELEVATION ·

0.48 m

10   0   10   20   30   40   cm

W

Z

Z

Y

Y

Z

0.55 m

1.21 m

PLAN LOOKING UP ·

PLAN OF TOP ·

B E N C H

G. ECKE DIREX   Y YANG DELIN
1937
IN THE POSSESSION OF THE AUTHOR

65

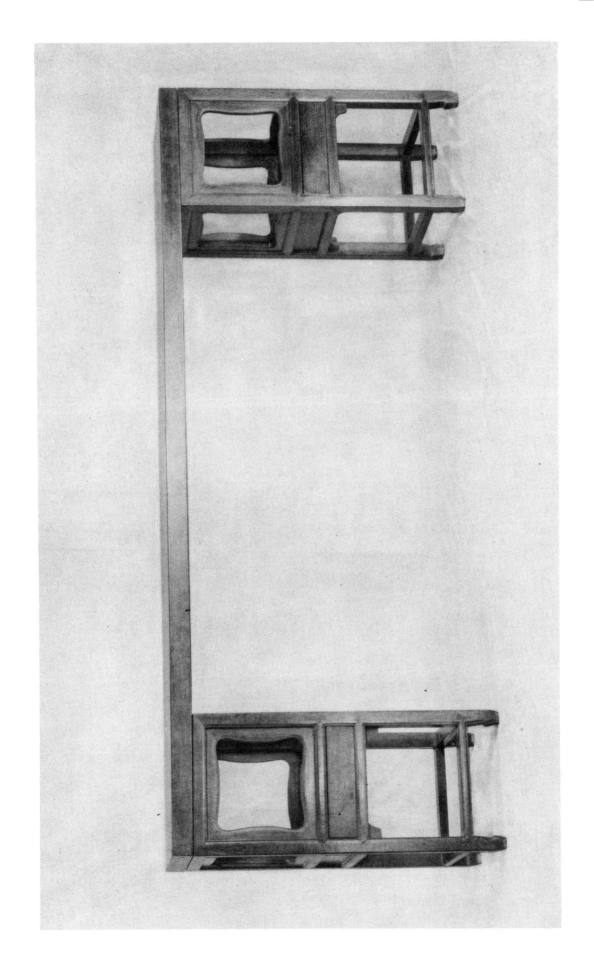

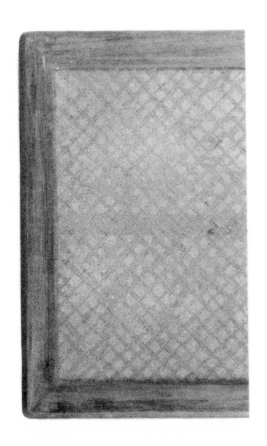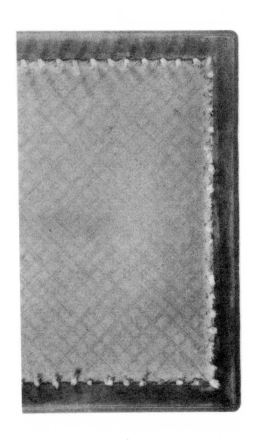

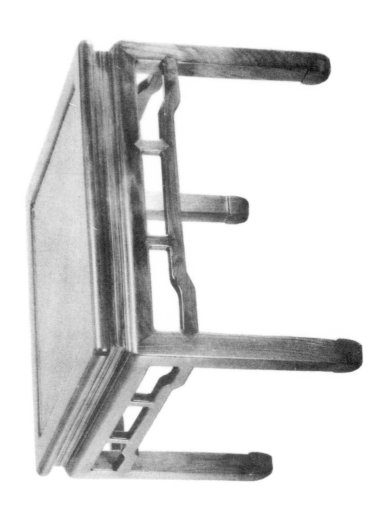

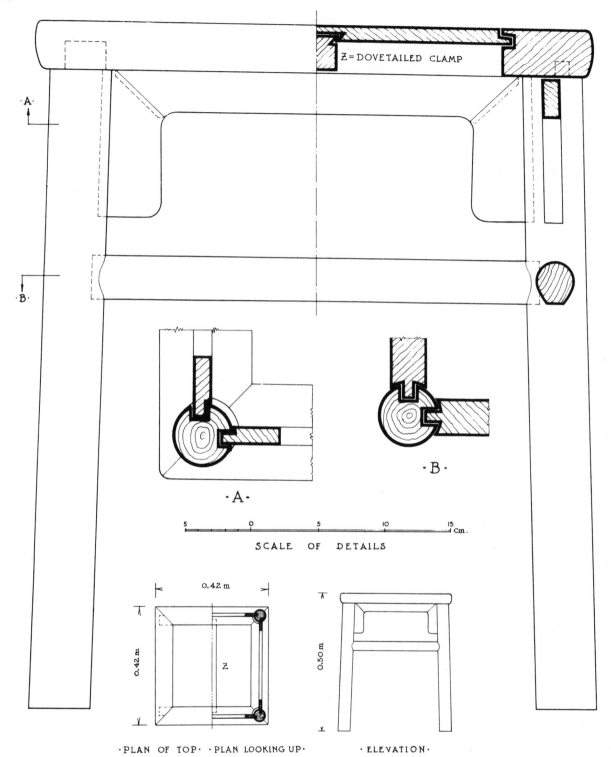

Z = DOVETAILED CLAMP

· A ·

· B ·

5   0   5   10   15 Cm.

SCALE OF DETAILS

0.42 m

0.42 m

Z

0.50 m

· PLAN OF TOP · · PLAN LOOKING UP ·   · ELEVATION ·

10 0 10 20 30 40 50 Cm.

STOOL

G. ECKE DIREX.   Y. YANG DELIN.

1934

IN THE POSSESSION OF THE AUTHOR

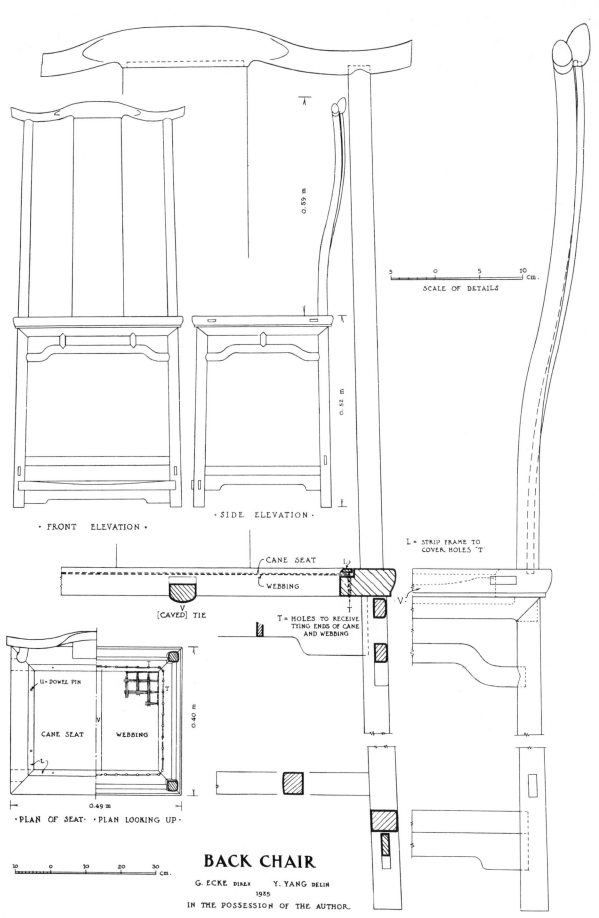

0.59 m

SCALE OF DETAILS

5   0   5   10 cm.

· FRONT ELEVATION ·

· SIDE ELEVATION ·

0.52 m

L = STRIP FRAME TO
COVER HOLES "T"

CANE SEAT

WEBBING

L

[CAVED] TIE

V

T = HOLES TO RECEIVE
TYING ENDS OF CANE
AND WEBBING

V

U = DOWEL PIN

T

CANE SEAT

WEBBING

0.40 m

V

L

0.49 m

· PLAN OF SEAT · PLAN LOOKING UP ·

10   0   10   20   30 cm.

BACK CHAIR

G. ECKE DIREX   Y. YANG DELIN
1935
IN THE POSSESSION OF THE AUTHOR

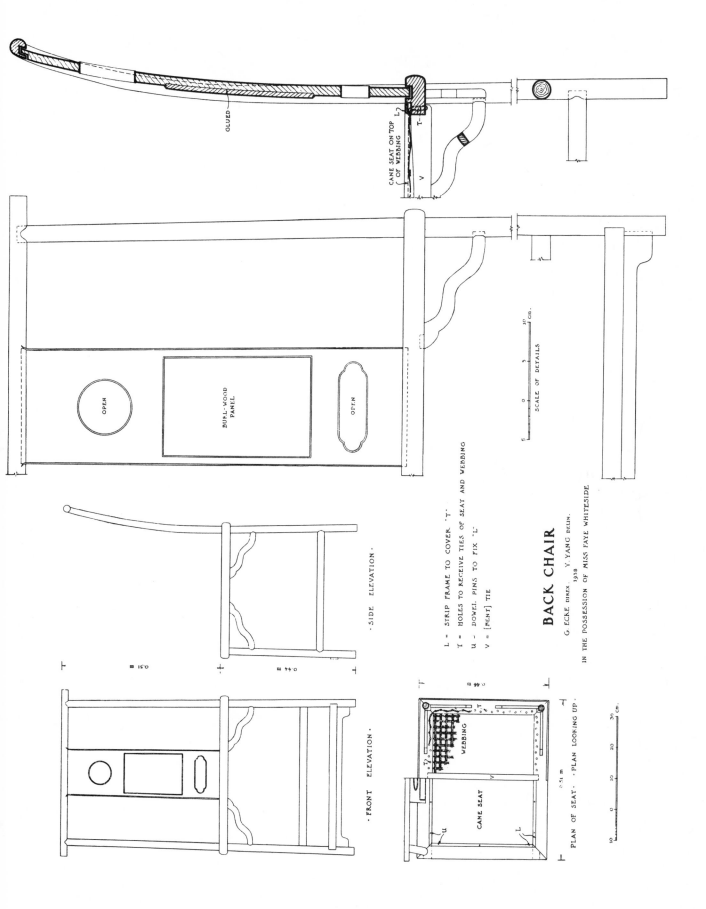

GLUED

CANE SEAT ON TOP
(OF WEBBING

OPEN

BULL-WOOD
PANEL

OPEN

10 CM.

SCALE OF DETAILS

· SIDE ELEVATION ·

L = STRIP FRAME TO COVER 'T'

T = HOLES TO RECEIVE TIES OF SEAT AND WEBBING

u = DOWEL PINS TO FIX 'L'

V = [PENT] TIE

BACK CHAIR

G. ECKE DIREX.   Y. YANG DELIN.
1938

IN THE POSSESSION OF MISS FAYE WHITESIDE

0.51 m

0.44 m

· FRONT ELEVATION ·

WEBBING

CANE SEAT

0.44 m

0.51 m

30 CM.

· PLAN OF SEAT ·   · PLAN LOOKING UP ·

82

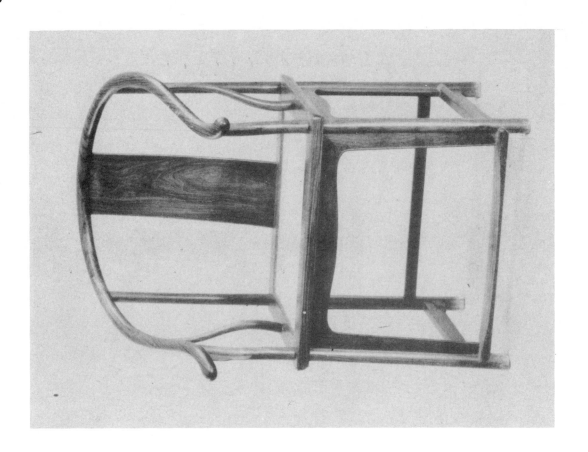

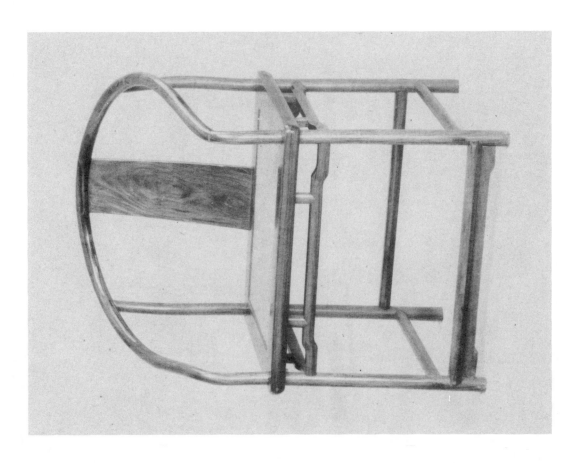

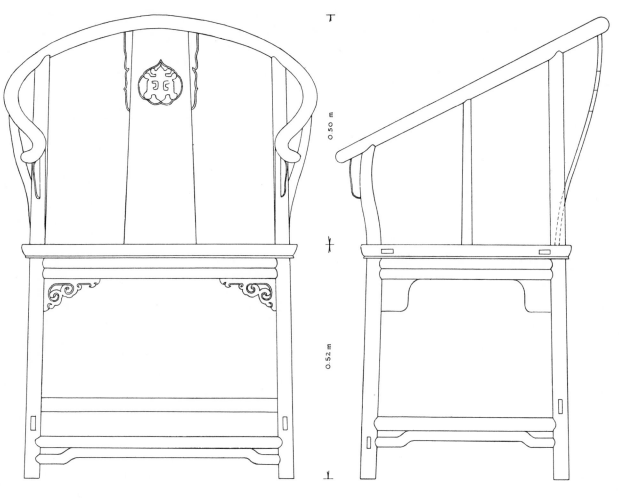

· FRONT ELEVATION ·   · SIDE ELEVATION ·

0.50 m

0.52 m

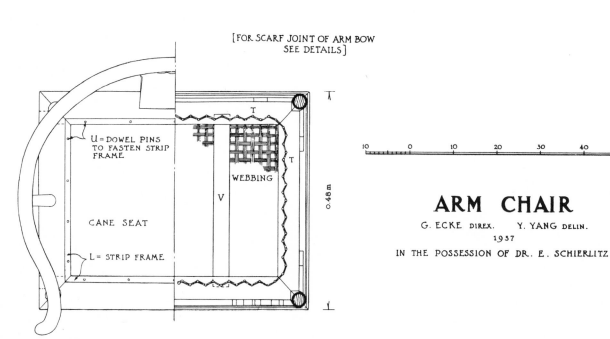

[FOR SCARF JOINT OF ARM BOW
SEE DETAILS]

U = DOWEL PINS
TO FASTEN STRIP
FRAME

WEBBING

CANE SEAT

L = STRIP FRAME

0.48 m

0.62 m

· PLAN OF SEAT ·   · PLAN LOOKING UP ·

10   0   10   20   30   40   50
                                      cm.

ARM CHAIR

G. ECKE DIREX.   Y. YANG DELIN.
1937
IN THE POSSESSION OF DR. E. SCHIERLITZ

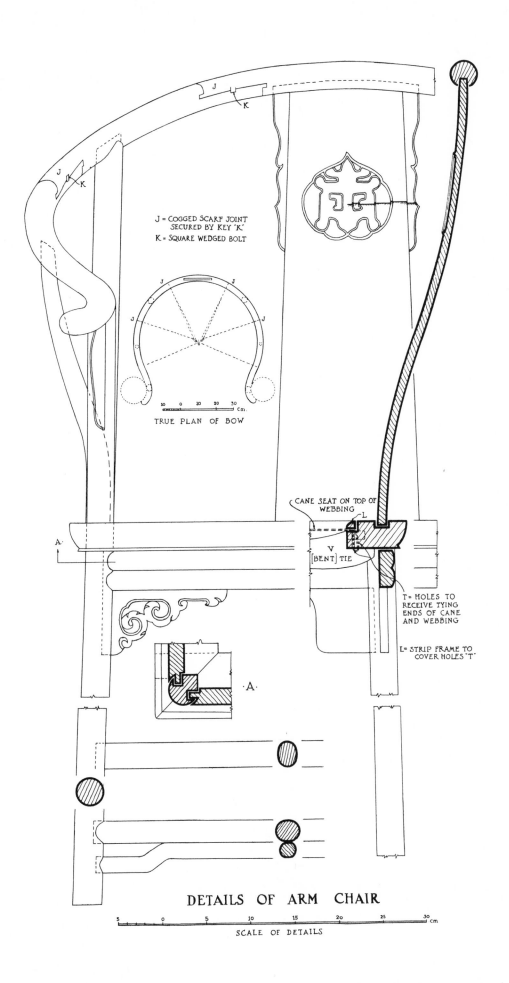

J = COGGED SCARF JOINT
SECURED BY KEY "K"

K = SQUARE WEDGED BOLT

TRUE PLAN OF BOW

CANE SEAT ON TOP OF
WEBBING

V
[BENT] TIE

T = HOLES TO
RECEIVE TYING
ENDS OF CANE
AND WEBBING

L = STRIP FRAME TO
COVER HOLES "T"

·A·

DETAILS OF ARM CHAIR

SCALE OF DETAILS

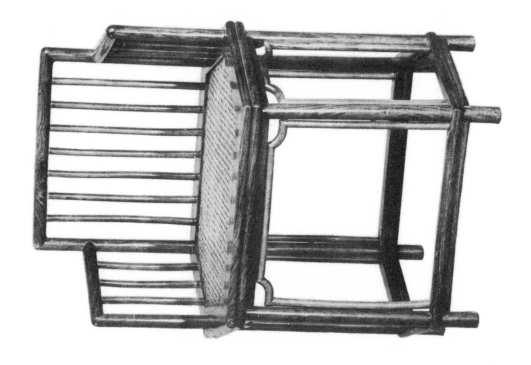

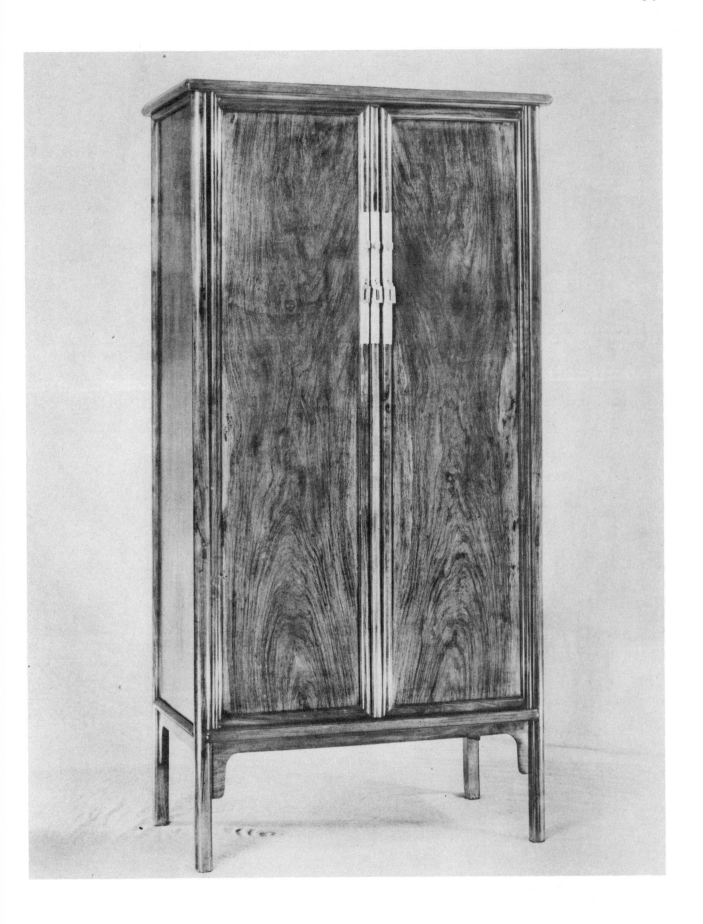

93,94

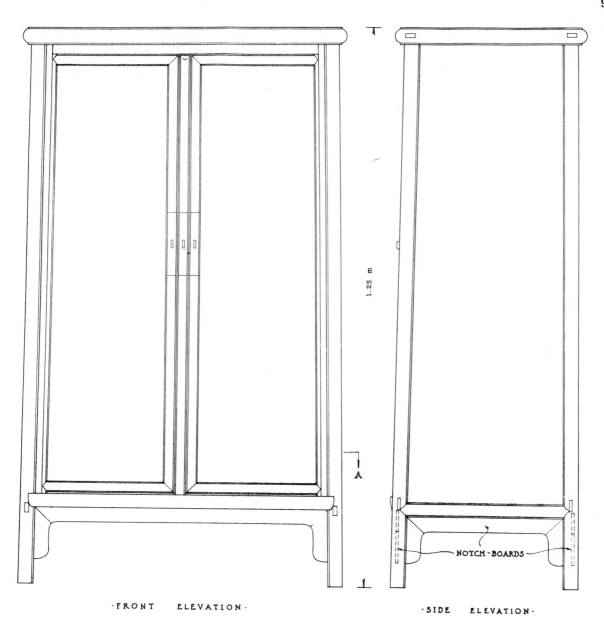

·FRONT ELEVATION·

·SIDE ELEVATION·

NOTCH-BOARDS

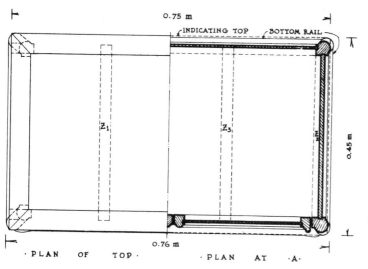

·PLAN OF TOP·

·PLAN AT ·A·

CABINET

G. ECKE DIREX. Y. YANG DELIN.
1935
IN THE POSSESSION OF THE AUTHOR

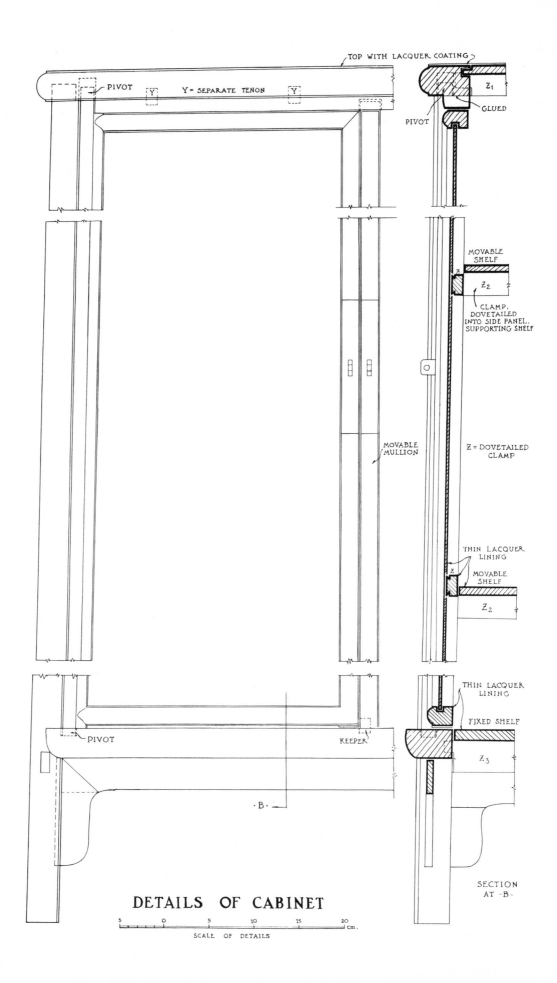

TOP WITH LACQUER COATING

PIVOT   Y   Y = SEPARATE TENON   Y

Z_1

GLUED

PIVOT

MOVABLE SHELF

Z_2

CLAMP,
DOVETAILED
INTO SIDE PANEL,
SUPPORTING SHELF

Z = DOVETAILED
CLAMP

MOVABLE
MULLION

THIN LACQUER
LINING

MOVABLE SHELF

Z_2

PIVOT   KEEPER

·B·

THIN LACQUER
LINING

FIXED SHELF

Z_3

SECTION
AT ·B·

DETAILS OF CABINET

SCALE OF DETAILS

97

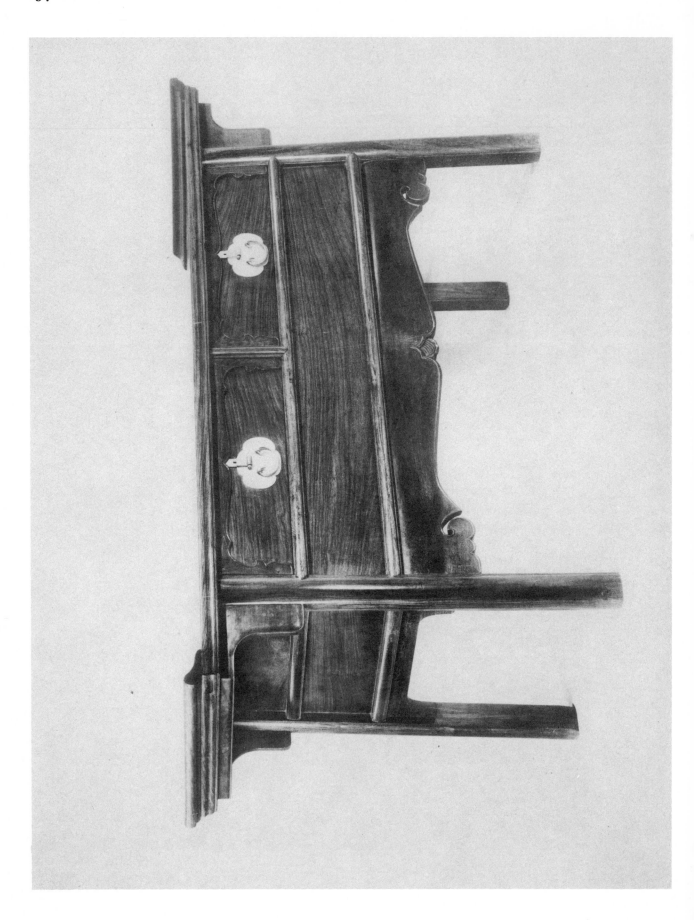

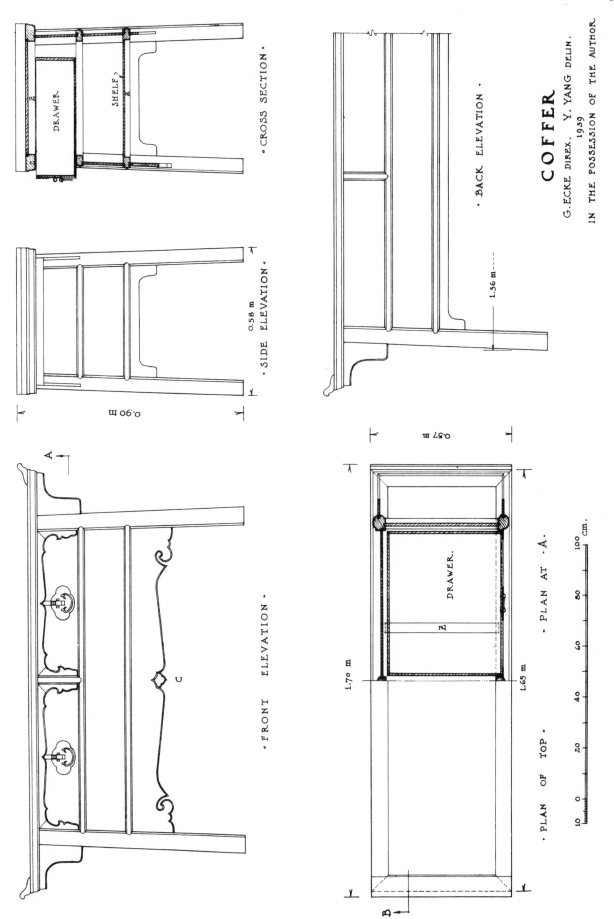

· CROSS SECTION ·

DRAWER.

SHELF?

· BACK ELEVATION ·

1.56 m

· SIDE ELEVATION ·

0.58 m

0.90 m

COFFER

G. ECKE DIREX. Y. YANG DELIN.
1939
IN THE POSSESSION OF THE AUTHOR.

· FRONT ELEVATION ·

C

A

B

· PLAN OF TOP ·

DRAWER.

· PLAN AT · A ·

1.70 m

1.65 m

0.57 m

10 0   20   40   60   80   100   CM.

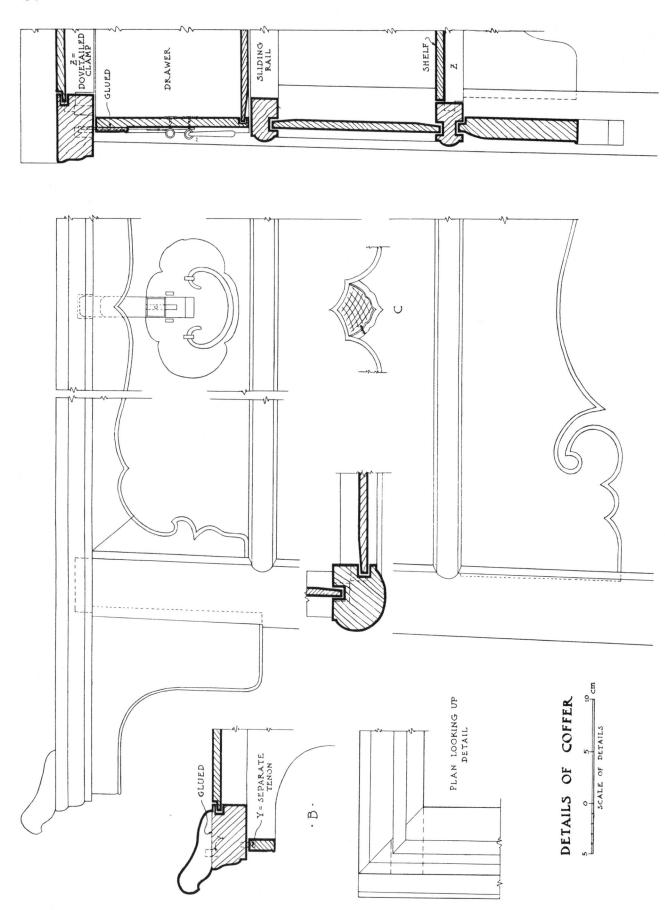

Z = DOVETAILED CLAMP

GLUED

DRAWER

SLIDING RAIL

SHELF

Z

C

GLUED

Y = SEPARATE TENON

·B·

PLAN LOOKING UP DETAIL

DETAILS OF COFFER

SCALE OF DETAILS

5   0   5   10 cm

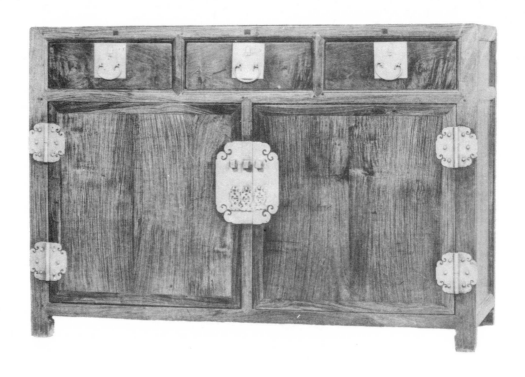

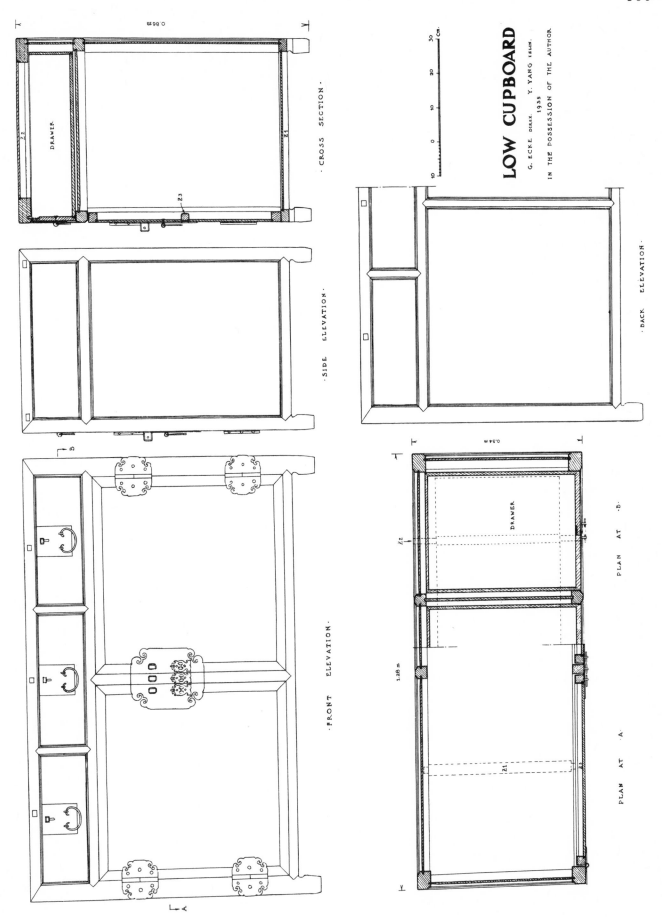

. CROSS SECTION .

DRAWER.

0.86 m

· SIDE ELEVATION ·

· FRONT ELEVATION ·

LOW CUPBOARD

G. ECKE DIREX.   Y. YANG DELIN.
1935
IN THE POSSESSION OF THE AUTHOR.

· BACK ELEVATION ·

DRAWER.

0.54 m

PLAN AT · B ·

1.28 m

PLAN AT · A ·

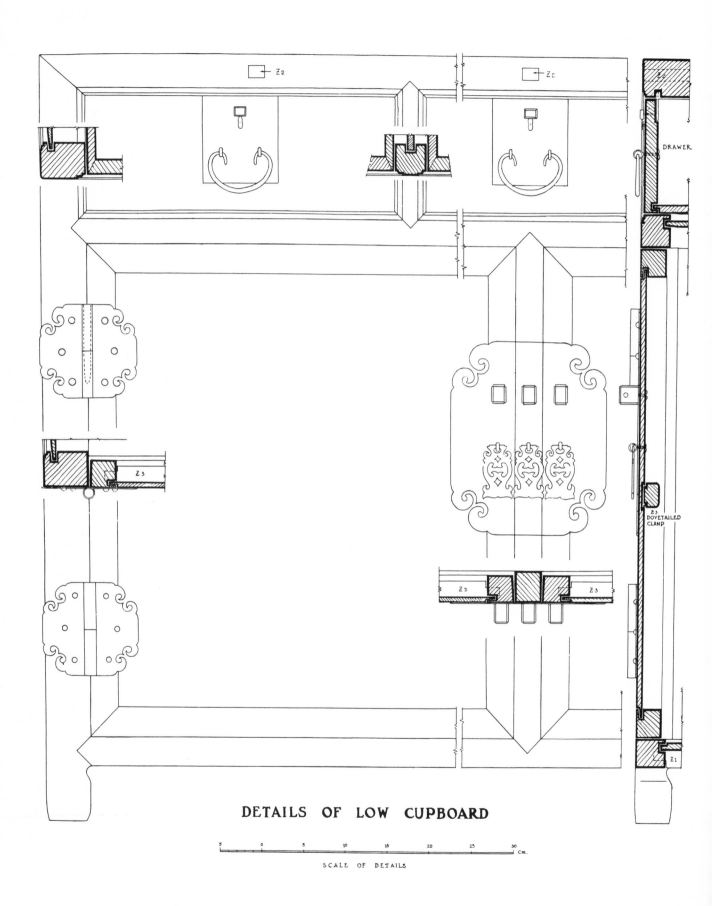

DETAILS OF LOW CUPBOARD

DRAWER

Z3
DOVETAILED
CLAMP

SCALE OF DETAILS

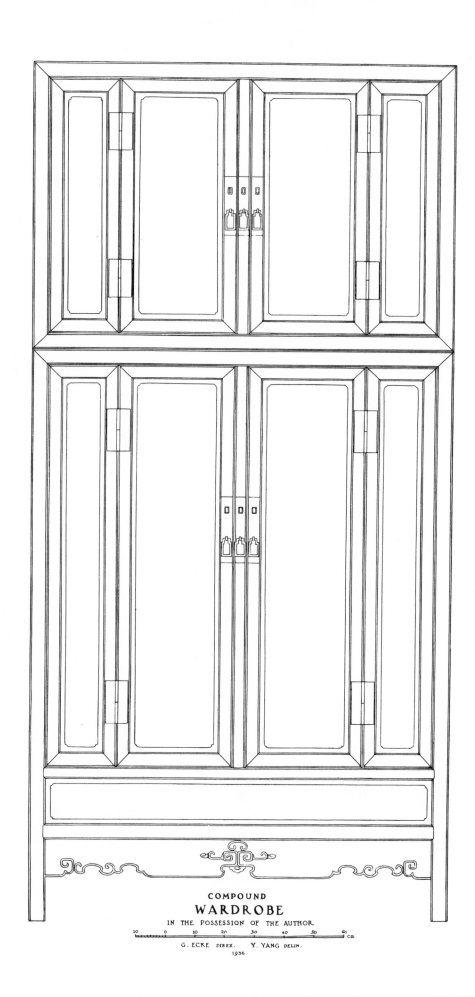

COMPOUND
WARDROBE
IN THE POSSESSION OF THE AUTHOR
G. ECKE DIREX.   Y. YANG DELIN.
1936

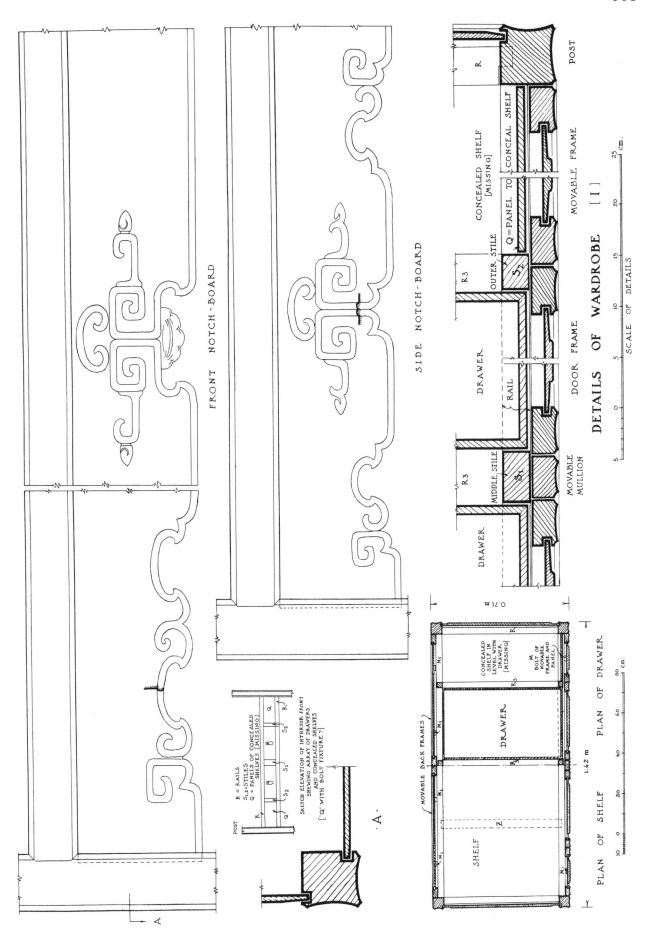

FRONT NOTCH-BOARD

SIDE NOTCH-BOARD

POST
R = RAILS
$S_{1,2}$ = STILES OF CONCEALED
Q = PANELS SHELVES [MISSING]

SKETCH ELEVATION OF INTERIOR FRONT
SHEWING ARRAY OF DRAWERS
AND CONCEALED SHELVES
['Q' WITH BOLT FIXTURE ?]

'A'

CONCEALED SHELF
[MISSING]

POST

Q = PANEL TO CONCEAL SHELF

MOVABLE FRAME

R_3

OUTER STILE

S_2

DRAWER

RAIL

DOOR FRAME

MIDDLE STILE

S_1

R_3

DRAWER

MOVABLE
MULLION

DETAILS OF WARDROBE [I]

SCALE OF DETAILS

cm.

MOVABLE BACK FRAMES

M_1

M

CONCEALED
SHELF IN
LEVEL WITH
DRAWER.
(MISSING)

R_3

BOLT OF
MOVABLE
FRAME AND
PANEL.

DRAWER

M_1

M

0.71 m

1.42 m

SHELF

Z

M

cm.

PLAN OF SHELF   PLAN OF DRAWER

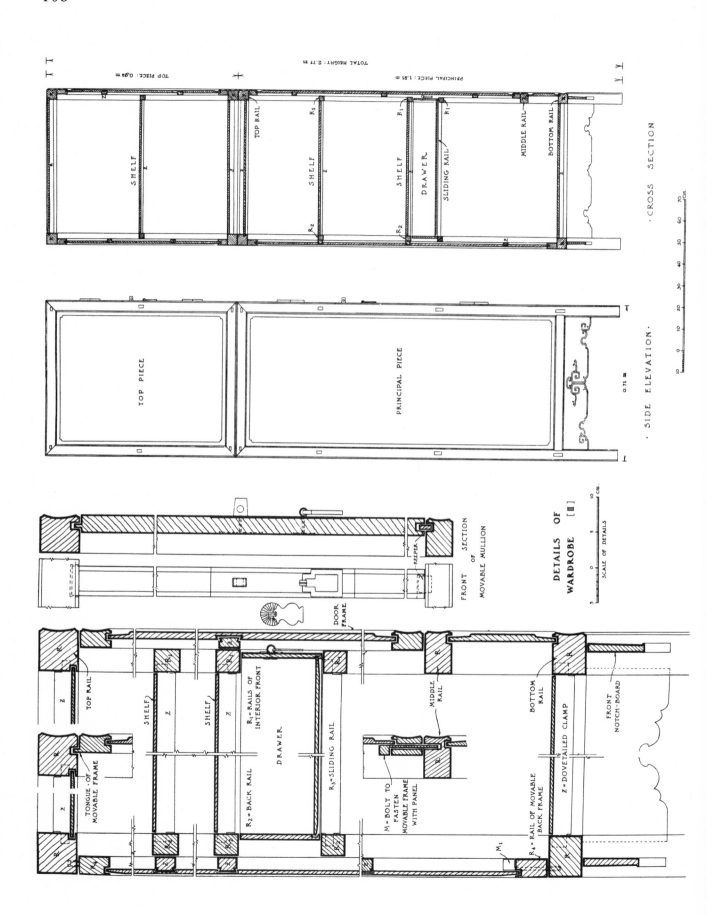

TOTAL HEIGHT: 2.77 m

TOP PIECE: 0.93 m.

PRINCIPAL PIECE: 1.85 m.

· CROSS SECTION ·

TOP RAIL

SHELF

SHELF

SHELF

DRAWER

SLIDING RAIL

MIDDLE RAIL

BOTTOM RAIL

· SIDE ELEVATION ·

0.71 m

TOP PIECE

PRINCIPAL PIECE

FRONT SECTION
OF
MOVABLE MULLION

KEEPER

DETAILS OF
WARDROBE [II]

SCALE OF DETAILS

DOOR
FRAME

TOP RAIL

TONGUE · OF ·
MOVABLE FRAME

SHELF

SHELF

R₁ = RAILS OF
INTERIOR FRONT

DRAWER

R₂ = BACK RAIL

R₃ = SLIDING RAIL

M = BOLT TO
FASTEN
MOVABLE FRAME
WITH PANEL

MIDDLE
RAIL

BOTTOM
RAIL

R₄ = RAIL OF MOVABLE
BACK FRAME

Z = DOVETAILED CLAMP

FRONT
NOTCH-BOARD

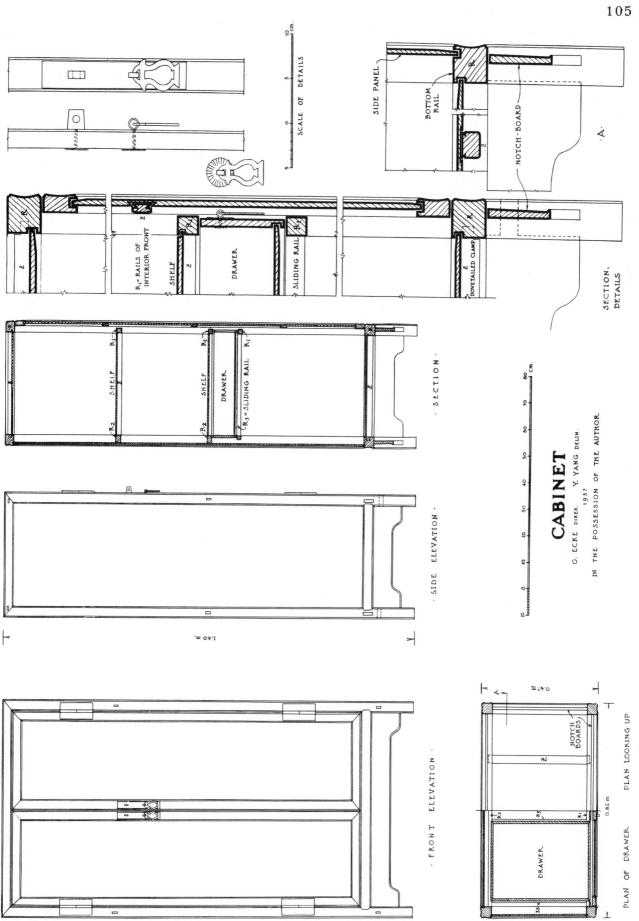

SCALE OF DETAILS

SIDE PANEL

BOTTOM RAIL

NOTCH-BOARD

·A·

SECTION, DETAILS

R₁ = RAILS OF INTERIOR FRONT

SHELF

DRAWER

SLIDING RAIL R₁

DOVETAILED CLAMP

·SECTION·

SHELF   R₁   R₁

R₂   SHELF   R₁

SHELF   R₁

DRAWER

R₃ = SLIDING RAIL

R₂

·SIDE ELEVATION·

1.60 m.

CABINET

G. ECKE DIREX.   V. YANG DELIN.
1937

IN THE POSSESSION OF THE AUTHOR

·FRONT ELEVATION·

·PLAN OF DRAWER·

DRAWER

NOTCH BOARDS

0.47 m

0.82 m

PLAN LOOKING UP

106

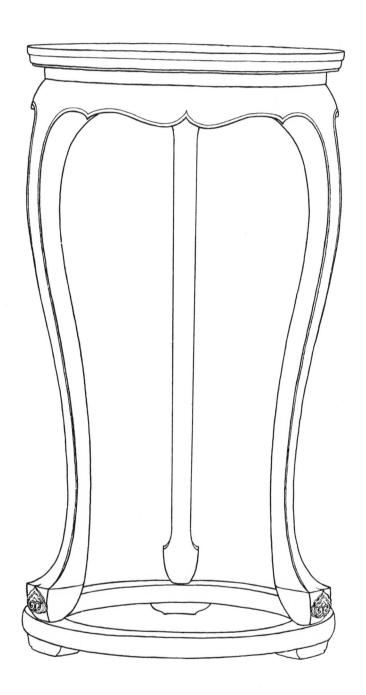

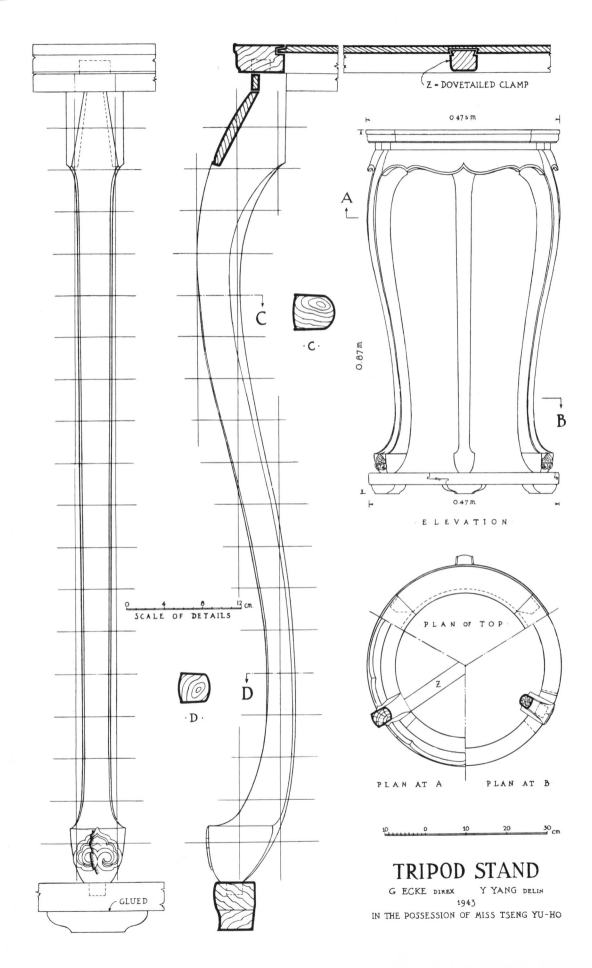

Z = DOVETAILED CLAMP

0.475 m

A

·C·

·D·

B

0.87 m

0.47 m

ELEVATION

0   4   8   12 cm.
SCALE OF DETAILS

PLAN OF TOP

Z

GLUED

PLAN AT A   PLAN AT B

10   0   10   20   30 cm

TRIPOD STAND

G ECKE DIREX   Y YANG DELIN
1943
IN THE POSSESSION OF MISS TSENG YU-HO

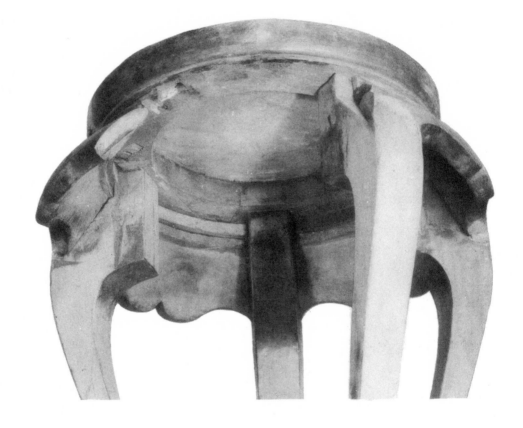

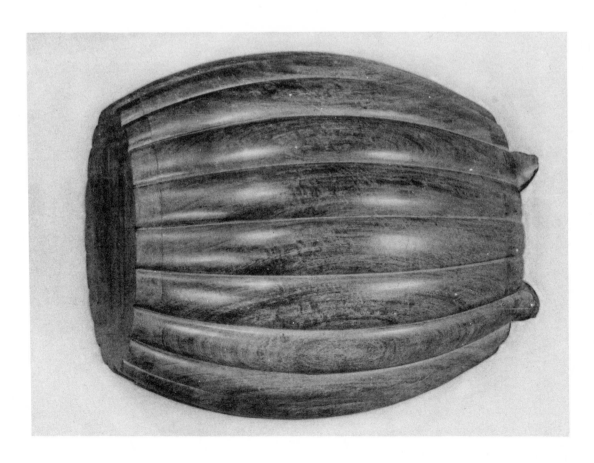

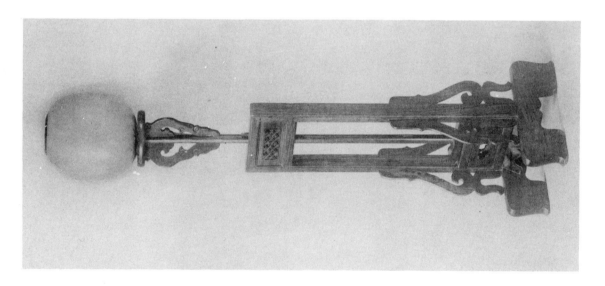

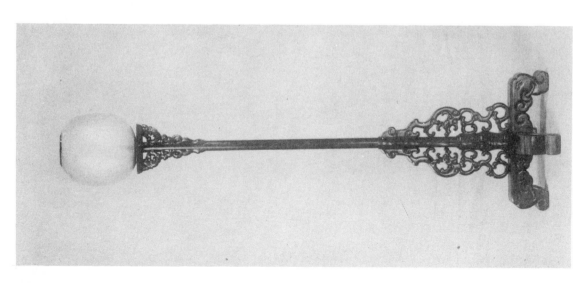

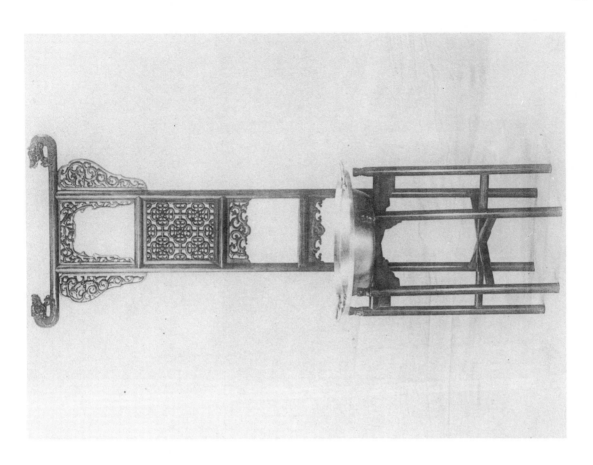

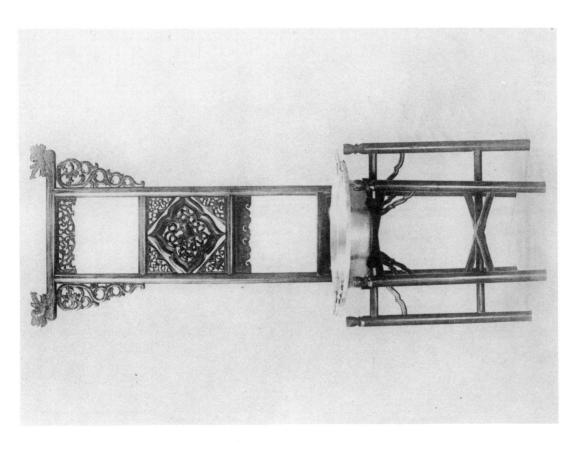

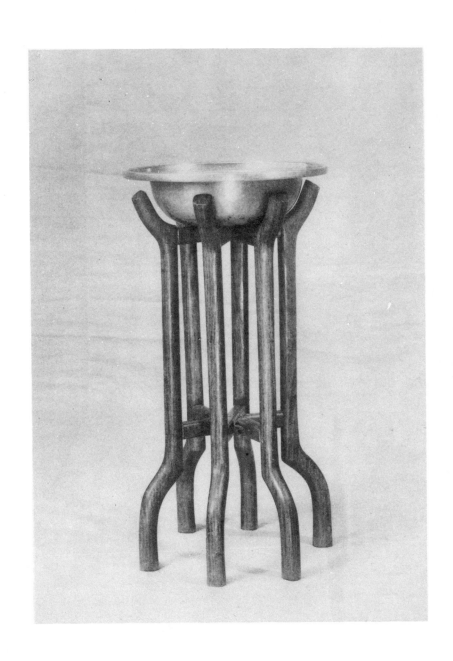

121

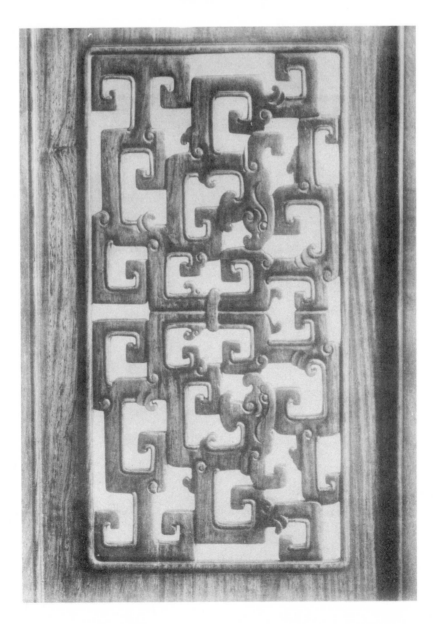

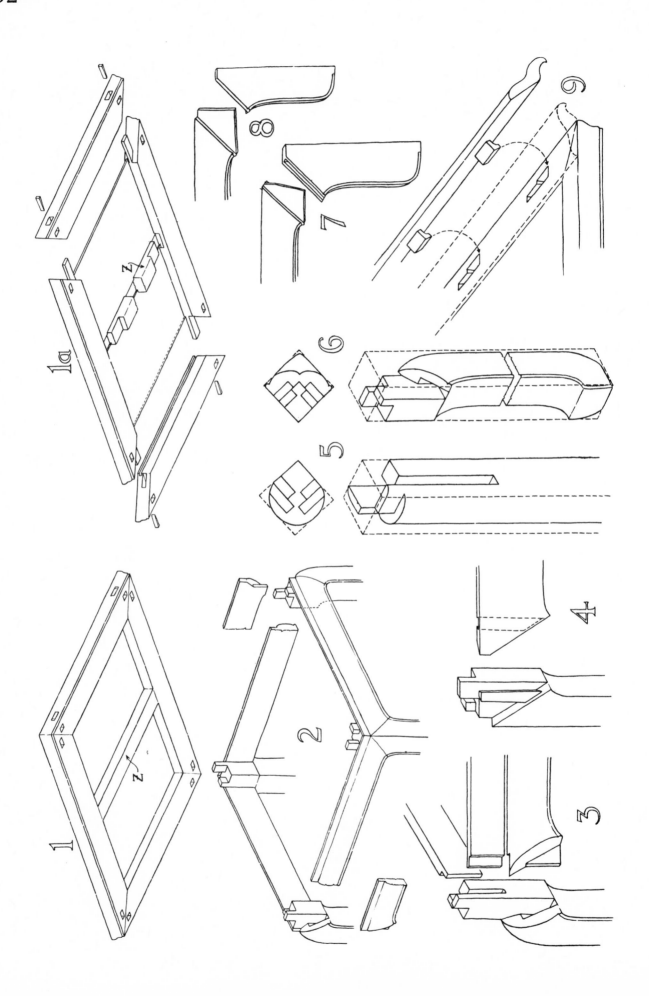

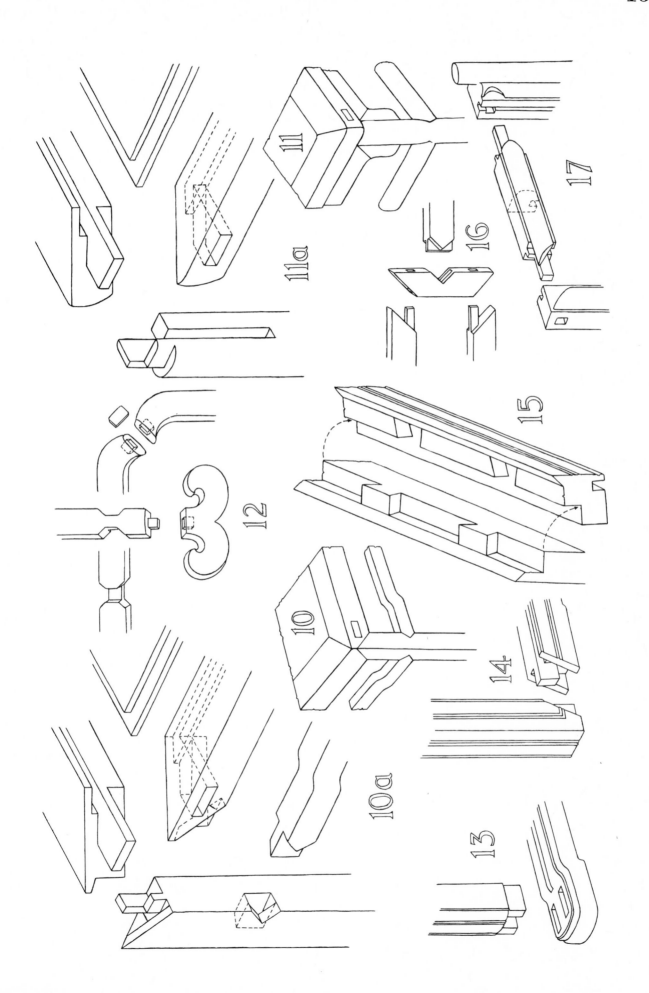

154

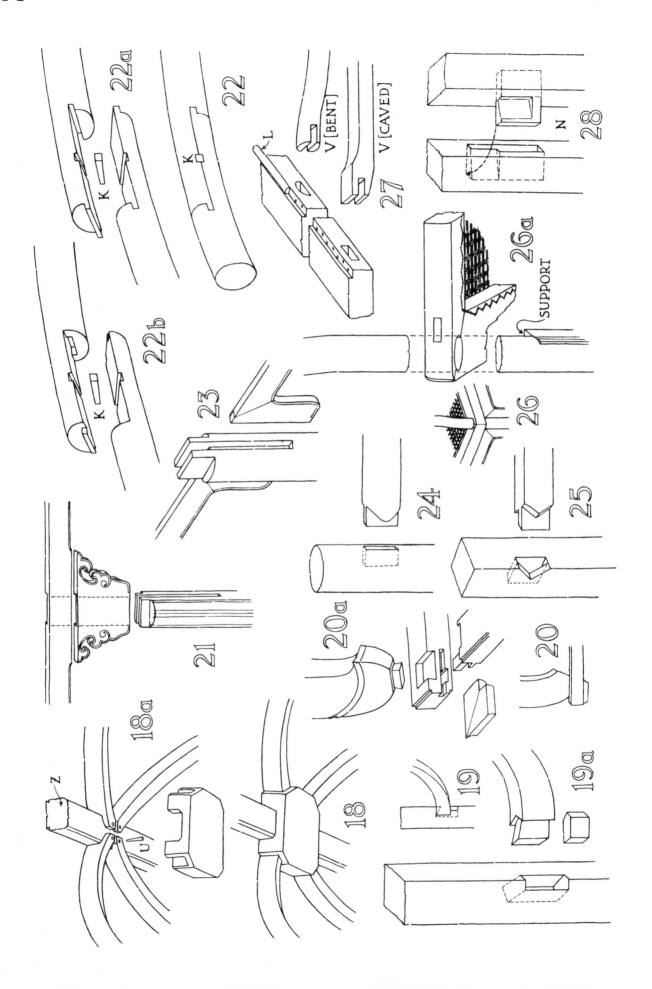

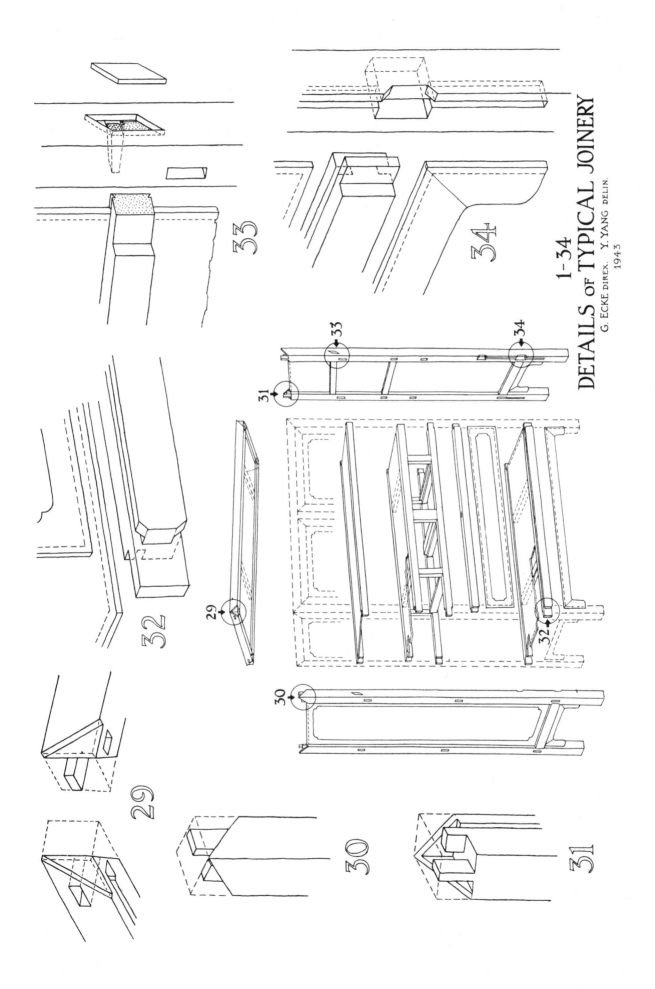

DETAILS of TYPICAL JOINERY

1-34

G. ECKE DIREX.   Y. YANG DELIN.

1943

101a, 101, 100,105

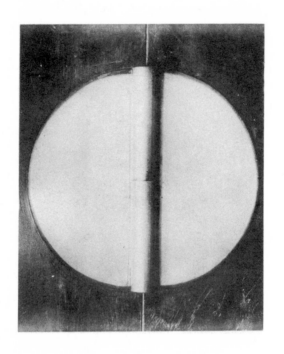

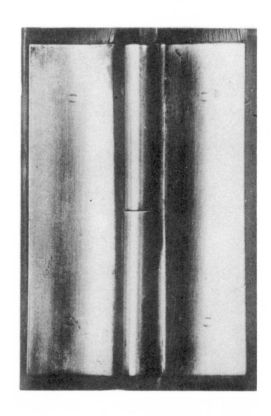

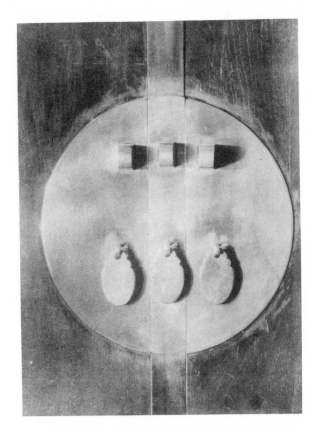

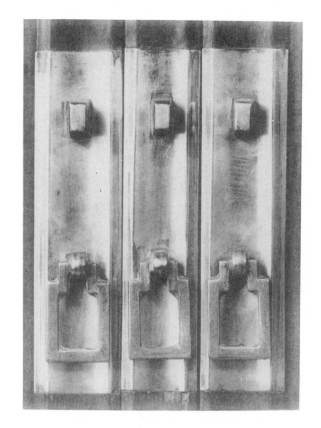

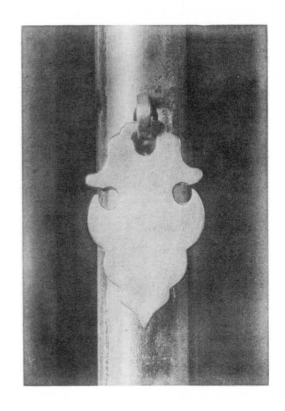

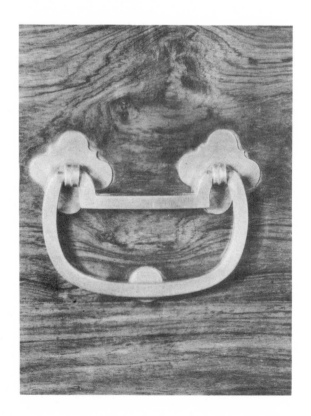